Emotionce

Build Strong Social Skills and Improve Your Relationships by Raising your EQ With Proven Methods and Strategies

Morten Johnson

Table of Contents

Introduction

It seems almost strange to think that the concept of emotional intelligence isn't well taught or even discussed in a lot of modern societies. In Western culture, specifically, young children are told to "keep their chin up" and not cry over the little things. Anger is considered a negative, explosive emotion that should never be expressed. Some of these biases are even used to target specific genders. Young boys and men are often chastised and teased for crying. The act becomes an emasculating scenario.

Interestingly enough, emotions are a vital part of humanity. Having a full range of emotions and being able to feel and express them is a near biological imperative that makes humans well, human. Take an individual who suffers from an antisocial personality disorder. One of the primary components of this disorder is not feeling remorse for their actions or compassion for the feelings of others. They are incapable of feeling that and are classified as having a disorder. Yet, people who allow themselves a full range of emotions are teased, told they are "too sensitive" or that they are weak.

It seems almost hypocritical, doesn't it? Unfortunately, the stigmas that surround the expression of emotions lead to individuals hiding their emotions, bottling them up, running from them, or flat out denying them. What is the harm in that, you ask? Well, unfortunately, bottling emotions, ignoring them, and denying them leads to a culture of emotionally stunted individuals who can't empathize, sympathize, or relate.

Alright, that's going a little too far ahead. Think of yourself as an emotional being. These emotions are directly linked to your behavior, thought patterns, and how you relate with others. By acknowledging emotions and expressing them in a healthy way, you give yourself self-awareness, you can manage your own life better, and you can manage relationships better. It is likely that your interest in emotional intelligence stems from a desire to improve certain aspects of your life that have been impacted by your own negative relationship with your own emotions.

When an emotion isn't properly expressed or felt, it becomes like water trapped in a dam. The pressure grows and grows as every situation you encounter while bottling up that emotion adds its own pressure to the dam. Finally, when the dam breaks, the emotional tidal wave that explodes can quite literally run roughshod all over your life. This is commonly seen in people with anger management or explosive anger issues. No emotion is immune to the proverbial dam they can get trapped behind. Unfortunately, when the tidal wave is unleashed, it is often over one single drop that broke the pressure. That drop might be small and insignificant, but the entire weight of the tidal wave comes out with it.

This means that a seemingly simple event can be the trigger and result in a much more catastrophic emotional release that has been building up for a long time. As a result, the person, or situation, that receives the brunt of the explosion might be completely undeserving of such an outburst. They just happened to be the final straw, or water drop to stay with the dam analogy, so to speak. These releases can then cause problems in your personal relationships, familial relationships, and even in your career and professional relationships.

It isn't just relationships that can be impacted by emotional intelligence. Performance in school or in your career, your physical and mental health, and your ability to socialize appropriately all hinge on your emotional intelligence.

So, what is to be done about it? Well, learning about emotional intelligence is the first step in gaining the upper hand and improving yourself. This book is going to be your starting point for knowledge and information about yourself as well as how you can improve your emotional intelligence. Despite what society tells you, you can empower yourself to live an emotionally healthier (and healthier overall) life.

Maybe you can't think of any specific situations that you might benefit from a higher EQ or EI (emotional intelligence). Here is a list of a few scenarios that can become much less stressful if you are aware of your own emotional intelligence:

- Meeting deadlines, especially tight, stressful ones

- Giving and receiving feedback

- Not having enough resources

- Dealing with difficult relationships

- Coping with change

- Handling setbacks and perceived failures

As you can see, many of these potential situations are quite broad. Therefore, emotional intelligence can be volatile in a wide range of areas in your life. With so many areas that emotional intelligence can help with, it seems like an obvious choice to begin working on your own emotional intelligence. That is why starting with *Emotional Intelligence: Build Strong Social Skills and Improve Your Relationships by Raising Your EQ With Proven Methods and Strategies* is going to be a vital tool in your personal transformation.

Harvard Business School did a comprehensive research study that's results determined EQ is vital to success. It was deemed twice as important than IQ and technical skills in determining who was successful (What is emotional intelligence? 2019, para 4).

Scientifically speaking, emotions are known to come before thoughts. Emotions can actually change the way the brain functions. They can impair the cognitive process, the ability to act interpersonally, and even inhibit the decision-making process.

Thankfully, emotional intelligence can be improved. Much like programming a computer, your mind and emotions can be "taught" or "programmed" to react a certain way. The emotional side of your brain and the rational side of your brain are separate. Emotional intelligence is based on how these two portions of your brain communicate. By improving their communication, you grow your emotional intelligence.

Your emotional intelligence pathway starts in the spinal cord of your nervous system. Before you can have a rational thought or reaction, your senses travel from the spinal cord directly into the front of the brain. Before these senses reach your rational brain, they pass through the limbic system, where emotions are generated. Biologically, emotions are triggered before rational thought (About emotional intelligence, 2020, para 11).

The human brain is essentially like a supercomputer, constantly processing information. The neural connections that allow you to process information and react are always changing and growing. When you learn new skills, acquire new information or knowledge, those connections change and grow. This is a lifelong process and is called plasticity (About emotional intelligence, 2020, para 12).

The process isn't instantaneous, though. It takes time for those connections to form and for the brain to begin processing information more efficiently across those new connections. This is why it is possible to improve your emotional intelligence, but also why it takes a certain level of commitment to make such a personal change.

That being said, having a higher emotional intelligence can quite literally change your life. Harvard Business School, a renowned and well-respected institute postured that EQ contributes to success! This can be career success, personal relationship success, or just reaching your personal goals in life. Consider what success means to you and what commitment you are willing to make to achieve it. All in all, reading this book and giving yourself new skills to carry with you through daily life isn't a very arduous commitment.

Imagine reaching all your goals and successes. It is a very elating, validating, and empowering vision, isn't it? Of course, it is! It should be. The opportunity that is presented within the chapters of this book is one that will help you bring that vision into reality. It might sound almost surreal, but the science and the methodology exists to show how beneficial EQ is to success. That is what *Emotional Intelligence* offers you, a chance, and the tools you need, to make your own success.

You've already taken your first step to changing. Just by purchasing and opening this book, you're on the path towards improving your emotional intelligence. Skills that you will learn about and improve are going to increase your self-awareness, improve your self-management, raise your mindfulness, help you with managing relationships, and increasing your social awareness. These major points impact everyone day to day, including you.

Now, to be clear, this is not a book on how to control your emotions or how to stop feeling certain emotions. EQ is all about managing emotions. That means learning how to express them appropriately, acknowledging the full range of human emotion, and applying them to the situations you are in throughout your daily life. It is about living with them in harmony. Understanding that will give you an advantage in relating to yourself and others.

It is never too late to decide that you are ready for a change, but has there ever been a better time than now? One of the factors that emotional intelligence creates ease around is change. Don't let your emotions hold you back this time. It is time to expand your emotional toolkit, starting right here with emotional intelligence.

Chapter 1:

What Is Emotional Intelligence and How Is It Different from IQ?

IQ vs. EQ

Many of you are probably familiar with IQ, or intelligence quotient. It is very possible that you've taken an IQ test before. If that is the case, then you already know what your IQ is. What is an IQ though, really? An IQ is the score given from a set of standardized tests that are designed to gauge an individual's intelligence. Traditionally, it is used to test a person's academic strengths and determine who has a higher than average intelligence or who might have mental challenges and learning disabilities.

Emotional intelligence (EI), or emotional quotient (EQ) consists of three parts. It is the ability to assess, identify, and evaluate the emotions of yourself, others, and groups of people. While IQ is based more on logical thinking, math skills, and spatial relations, EQ is a bit more complex. Not only is it about identifying and expressing your own emotions, but it also means perceiving and understanding someone else's emotions. People with a high EQ can channel emotions and use them in a way to get others to think more profoundly.

As you can see, IQ is geared more towards an individual's intelligence and academics problem-solving. On the flip side, EQ is more about understanding yourself through emotions, thoughts, and behaviors, as well as applying that same understanding to other people you come into contact with.

Being able to connect with other people in that emotional way is what leads people with high EQ to more success than people with high IQ.

Let's look at an example of two people in the workplace. One individual, we'll call him Spencer, has an incredibly high IQ. He is off the charts smart, certifiably a genius, and incredibly logical and technical. Spencer has a low EQ though. He is valued in the company because of his brilliance, but he has difficulty relating to and communicating with his coworkers. As a result, a lot of people see him as a "know it all." This leads Spencer to retreat further into himself and he becomes almost a recluse at work. He sticks to his own office or cubicle, doesn't eat lunch with his coworkers in the lunchroom. During work meetings he is always taking notes, but he sits in the back, and only ever speaks out if a fact is misspoken. He doesn't know how to support his peers if they are struggling with personal issues, and he comes off as awkward and uncomfortable if he tries. All of this is because Spencer has a low EQ.

Now, take a look at Emily. She has an average IQ and is no smarter or more accomplished than any of her peers. Yet, Emily has a high EQ. She socializes with her coworkers on breaks, even hosts after hours gatherings to instill team building with people she is working on projects with. Emily can assess when a coworker is struggling personally and professionally, and she will reach out to that person, offering whatever support she can. In work meetings, she is right in the center of everything, asking questions, offering her opinion, and giving feedback that takes many different angles into consideration which gets her employers and superiors interested and thinking about what she says. She has the ability to make her coworkers and peers feel comfortable around her, and she isn't afraid or shy when it comes to talking to them.

Imagine that both Spencer and Emily apply for a management position within the company to manage the "tools and tech" team. Spencer has the IQ and the know how to handle any situation that could arise from a technical standpoint on that team. However, Emily has the ability to better manage and handle the employees. She is someone that her team would feel comfortable approaching, someone who would support them and work on making the entire team stronger.

You can see why Emily would be favored for that position even though she isn't as technologically inclined as Spencer. In order to succeed in a workforce made of people, you need a certain amount of emotional intelligence. Think back on any job you've had before and consider situations where one person was promoted and another wasn't, even if both seemed equally qualified. Try to differentiate the EQ skills of both of them and see if that played a role in who was selected. You might even be surprised to find that you were passed over for a position you thought you were qualified for based on your EQ.

This anecdote is not designed to place biases. Both men and women can have high and low IQs. Both men and women can have high and low EQs. It is also not an attempt to separate introverts from extroverts. EQ has nothing to do with an individual's sociability. Both introverts and extroverts can have high or low EQ. While it might seem like Spencer and Emily in the above scenario differ socially, in this instance, it is due to Spencer having a low EQ and Emily having a high EQ.

Of course, EQ is more complex than just being social and relating to other people. Emily's willingness to support and engage with coworkers, her desire to create team building exercises and a communal atmosphere, as well as her questions that facilitated a thought-provoking reaction from her superiors are also what set her apart. These components are a part of EQ as well.

What Are Emotions?

The Merriam-Webster dictionary defines emotions as a conscious mental reaction subjectively experienced as strong feeling usually directed toward a specific subject and typically accompanied by physiological and behavioral changes in the body.

Another, less complicated definition that the dictionary provides is simply a state of feeling.

Emotions occur in the limbic system. This part of the brain is where the initial response to stimuli happens. The emotions take form before the rest of the brain can react to a specific stimulus. As chaotic, overwhelming, and even encumbrance emotions can seem, they are very important to humanity as a whole, as well as individuals.

Personally, emotions are linked directly to thoughts and behavior. They can influence your decisions and responses. These decisions can be as simple as what you want for breakfast or as large as where you want to go to college. Responses dictated by emotions might be as simple as rolling your eyes in annoyance. A more extreme reaction could be slamming a door in anger, or crying in sadness. Emotions can be short and fleeting or long-term and lasting.

A short emotion could be annoyance at your spouse or partner for leaving the toilet seat up after they use the bathroom. Long term emotions can come in the form of grief over the loss of a loved one, or even grudges that stem from anger.

Emotions are broken down into three different parts. There is a subjective component, meaning how you experience the emotion personally. The next part of an emotion is the physiological component. In other words, how your body experiences the emotion and reacts to it. The third component of emotions is expression. This refers to how you behave in response to that emotion.

So, why do people need emotions? Emotions, despite the stigmas that surround them, are incredibly important to everyday life.

Benefits and importance of emotions include:

- Emotions provide motivation to take action

- Emotions help you survive, thrive, and avoid danger

- Emotions assist in decision making

- Emotions allow other people to understand you

- Emotions allow you to understand other people

As a social species, understanding other humans and being understood is a vital part of communication. You've probably experienced the frustration at trying to explain something to someone else and them not understanding you. It can be incredibly vexing to have that problem. Think of your emotions the same way. If no one understood how you felt, that would be incredibly painful and irritating. It would cause you to feel very alone and isolated. Humans strive for connection and belonging because they are social.

There are many ways that emotions benefit individuals and the human species as a whole.

There are six core or basic emotions that every human is prone to feeling. Those six emotions are:

- Happiness

- Sadness

- Fear

- Disgust

- Anger

- Surprise

All of these emotions can be expressed through facial features, body posture, and vocalizations. The body will also experience a physiological response, however it is not always a response that can be seen by others.

Happiness is usually expressed through smiling, a relaxed posture, and an upbeat tone of voice.

Sadness can usually be indicated through the action of crying, having a sullen demeanor, being tired and lethargic, a quiet voice or not saying much at all, and being withdrawn from others.

Disgust presents physically as turning away or moving away from the source of the reaction. When you are disgusted, you might gag, heave, retch, or vomit. Your face might scrunch up with a wrinkled nose or curling back the upper lip.

Fear can be seen in the face with wide eyes and the chin pulling back. Body language shows the desire to run and/or hide from whatever is causing the fear. An increased heartbeat, rapid breathing, and perspiration can also be indicators of fear.

Anger is usually present on the face as scowling or glaring. The lips often form down in a frown. The body language becomes somewhat hostile, turning away from the source of anger or taking a strong, firm stance. Verbally, anger comes out in gruffness, roughness, and sometimes yelling. It might even manifest as excessive sarcasm. When the body feels anger it will often turn red, or begin to sweat. In extreme cases, anger can turn into an aggressive outburst that results in hitting, kicking, biting, throwing things, and other violent acts.

Surprise manifests in a dropped jaw, raised eyebrows, and widening of the eyes. A physical response from surprise can be jumping or the entire body startling. When you are surprised, your verbal response might be yelling, gasping, or screaming.

You have most likely experienced all of these emotions at one point in your life. You've probably noticed the physical, physiological, facial, verbal, and body posture responses to all of these emotions. It is possible that you've seen them present in other people. Maybe your responses are slightly different, but you can still relate which responses correlate to these emotions.

The interesting thing about emotions is that you can experience combined emotions. Meaning you could be surprised and fearful at the same time. Or, you could be sad and angry at the same time. You could even be happy and sad at the same time. When you combine two basic emotions, you can end up with a more complex emotion. Take the basic emotions of sadness and disgust. Combine them together, and you get the complex emotion of remorse. If you combine surprise and fear, you get the more complicated emotion of awe.

Just like a color wheel with primary colors that can be mixed to make secondary colors and so on, emotions can be combined for more in-depth feelings. Have you picked up on the complexity of emotions and how vital they are to human interaction and success yet?

EQ in Detail

Emotional intelligence is broken into a few key parts. These components will be elaborated on continuously in the chapters to come, however knowing their break down is going to give you a starting point for your progression through understanding and increasing your own EQ.

In Chapters 4 and 5 these key components will be split up. You will be given tools and exercises to apply to these components that will help you increase your EQ. You'll notice that the different components of your emotional intelligence intertwine and build off of each other to be applied in different situations.

Self-Awareness

Self-awareness in regard to emotional intelligence relates specifically to your ability to perceive your own emotions. It is more than just knowing what your emotions are though. It is also about remaining aware of them while they are happening. Knowing your emotions after they are experienced only gets you so far. Hindsight doesn't give you an advantage going forward. So, when it comes to self-awareness, it is being aware of your emotions as they happen and the reactions you have with those emotions.

For example, every time you go into the break room at work, there is an empty soda can left on the table where people eat their lunches. You storm out of the break room, mumbling under your breath and complaining to your coworkers about how unclean the break room is. Maybe you even grind your teeth and internally vow to find out who keeps messing up the break room. It can ruin your entire mood at work.

Once the irritation dissipates, you are able to determine that an empty soda can left on the break room table is bothersome to you. It is unsanitary for someone to leave an item they put their mouth and saliva all over on the same table that other people will be eating their lunches at. You are irritated, but you are also disgusted by the uncleanliness. In the moment you felt irritation, but when you looked back, you were able to determine the irritation stemmed from disgust. This is the first step to being self-aware.

Being aware of your emotions and where they originate from is only half of self-awareness. Now that you've identified the source, the next time you see that soda can, you'll be able to acknowledge that seeing it is going to make you feel disgusted. In knowing that, you can prepare yourself to have a conscious reaction, rather than defaulting to irritation. You'll be able to acknowledge the disgust in the moment, but prevent it from ruining the rest of your day by devolving into irritation.

Self-Management

Being able to self-manage your emotions stems directly from being aware of them. Self-management, in reference to EQ, is about taking that awareness of your emotions and managing it in a productive way. Essentially, you use your self-awareness to be flexible with your emotional responses and to channel them in a positive way that results in positive behavior. You don't let your emotions control you because you can manage how you react.

Let's go back to the soda can in the breakroom. Now that you've identified the source of your irritation and the response you have, you can take it one step further and come up with a positive way to channel that expression. Maybe you'll put a sign on the break room wall over the table where the soda can is left every day saying something like, "Please keep our break room clean and properly dispose of your trash and empty food containers."

A generic message doesn't single anyone out or escalate the situation. It addresses the issue and the underlying irritation without pointing blame or making it a personal gripe that only you have. You avoid ruining your whole day and feel better about releasing that emotional energy.

Social-Awareness

Having social-awareness is a step away from focusing on your own emotions. When you step into social-awareness, you are able to perceive the emotions of other people you are coming into contact with. Over time, you learn to understand the people that you are closest to, but high EQ comes with being able to understand people that you pass on the street casually. You'd be surprised how many people in an emotional tailspin respond positively to a stranger reaching out with a semblance of understanding. That kind of kindness and compassion can change your life, and theirs.

Handling Relationships

Building off of social awareness, using your EQ to handle relationships is when you are aware of your own emotions as well as the emotions of the other person involved. Going beyond simple awareness, you can then use both parties' emotions to manage the situation. This can be beneficial in de-escalating arguments, showing support during grief, and helping reduce your partner's stress over house chores. Handling relationships isn't just in regard to romantic relationships either. It applies to all kinds of relationships you have, familial, friend, romantic, parental, even professional.

Empathy

Empathy is the ability to relate to another person. More than that, it is the ability to share emotions with another person. A lot of people think that you can't properly empathize with someone if you haven't been through the exact same situation as them. The word sympathy often relates to two people sharing feelings over a common experience.

It is important to differentiate these two words and types of relationships. They are too often used interchangeably. With a high EQ, it is quite possible to relate to another's emotions and to share an emotion with them without going through the same experience. This is empathy.

For example, a friend of yours loses their brother in a car crash. You are a single child. You don't know what it is like to have a brother or lose a brother. You've never known anyone that died in a car crash. Does that prevent you from sharing your friend's grief or being a support for them while they grieve? It shouldn't. You should be able to share in their pain just by understanding the emotions of grief and pain. That is empathy.

If your friend broke up with their long-time partner two years after you went through a divorce, then being able to share that pain from a similar experience would classify as sympathy.

Now, not all experiences where emotions can be empathized with are painful grievous experiences. They were used as examples as people, as a whole, tend to have more difficulty relating to a friend or family member suffering from loss.

Emotions like happiness can also be shared, as can anger, surprise, trust, love, etc. Just because emotions can be shared doesn't mean that you have to experience emotions the same as the person who is feeling it. You can still empathize and be supportive without crying alongside your friend at their brother's funeral. You can still show empathy when your child gets their driver's license by expressing your joy and excitement, even if you don't jump up and down like they do.

So, an important part of empathy is acknowledging that everyone experiences emotions differently. This is where EQ ties into empathy more deeply. Yes, you need a certain level of EQ to be able to empathize at all. You also need a higher level of EQ to express your empathy in a way that is received well, even if it is in a different way than other people are expressing theirs. You'll also need a higher level of EQ to know when you are receiving empathy from someone who processes and expresses emotion differently than you.

Despite humans being emotional and social creatures, humans are still individuals. This understanding is going to be a driving force in growing your EQ as well as applying your skills to yourself and everyone around you. Your goal is not to increase your emotional intelligence in order to force or convince others to conform to your emotional responses. There is a certain level of acceptance that everyone and their emotional responses are different that comes from a high EQ. That, in itself, is an empathetic quality.

The Connection Between Thoughts, Emotions, and Behaviors

As described previously, your emotions manifest physically and physiologically. They can impact your thoughts and thought process as well as your behaviors and actions. Not all actions and behaviors are socially acceptable. Now, this is going to vary greatly depending on your culture and geographical region. In order to be successful and raise your EQ, you need to have a good understanding of what kind of behaviors are acceptable and what aren't. This can also change over time and based on political leaders. Having a high EQ is going to give you the ability to adapt your emotional responses through various changes.

Looking at the interrelated relationship between emotion, thought, and behavior, you'll see how each one has such a strong impact. Using an example from a cognitive behavioral paradigm, imagine the outside stimulus of a project deadline being moved up by three days. You already had the workload spread out in a way that utilized those additional three days.

The moment that you get the news that your deadline was moved up, the first thought that runs through your mind is, "I'm never going to get this done." Since emotions are processed faster than rational thought, you immediately become panicked and anxious. Your body begins to respond physically with a loss of appetite, heart palpitations and muscle tenseness. Your behavior changes. You begin to pace and stutter instead of working. You become irritable.

This cycle becomes a vicious circle. The more you pace and lose focus, the less work you get done. This brings you right back to the initial thought of, "I'm never going to get this done." Your anxiety and panic rises, leading to more physical debilitations. Now, you're irritable because you haven't been eating and because you are anxious. You're getting yourself deeper into this whole of not getting your work done which feeds the muscle tension and anxiety. It goes round and round, your thought, emotion, behavior, and physical responses overlapping and continuing to exacerbate the situation by contributing to each other.

This cycle can happen in any number of ways. It is possible that you hear your deadline is moved up and you immediately jump to panic and worry. That leads to irritability, which leads to a lack of appetite. Not eating makes you irritable, and finally you come to the conclusion that you won't get your work done.

Regardless of where your reaction begins, whether it is with a thought, feeling, or behavior, it becomes a leapfrog effect, until all three are connected to that single external stimulus.

Now, you might naturally default to a thought reaction. Someone else might default to a behavior reaction. Better understanding how you process information and what follows that processing is going to help you raise your EQ. Remember the last time you got really good news. Think about what your initial response was. Were you bursting with joy? Did you first think about what great news it was? Did you jump up and down giddily and hug the person who gave you the news?

The answer might be different for you depending on the situation and the emotional inclination. What that means is, you might react physically initially to good news. For bad news, you might have an emotional initial reaction. The complexities of these emotional patterns are boundless. When you get a handle on understanding your own, and in perceiving other people's, it is clear to see how important these skills are to success.

Emotions, thoughts, and behaviors are linked in many ways. When it comes to decision making, emotions play a key role. Your emotions can drive your thoughts, which then lead you to the behavior that comes with the decision you choose. Every time you make a choice, take an action, perform a behavior, or have a thought, there is an emotional component. No matter how pronounced or discrete it is. Whenever you experience an emotion, there is a thought and behavior that contribute to your emotional response. Any time you have a certain behavior, there are thoughts and emotions that contribute to your behavioral patterns.

Rather than trying to separate emotion, thought, and behavior in an attempt to control or suppress yourself, the best way to handle this interconnectedness is to change the way you react and respond. Consider yourself lightning. It is easier to redirect lightning with a lightning rod than it is to try and stop a thunderstorm from forming in the first place. Behavior, thought, and emotion are all types of body chemistry and thus body energy. In chemistry, you have to have the right mix of ingredients to get the desired outcome. Removing one piece changes the compound completely.

In order to raise your EQ, you really have to understand how these parts of yourself are connected and how they interact. Take some time to write down a few experiences where you can vividly recall your reactions emotionally, behaviorally, and cognitively. Begin to work out for yourself your connections and reactions. It is going to be greatly beneficial as you progress through future chapters.

Chapter 2:

Why Emotional Intelligence Is

Crucial for Success

What is it about EQ that makes such a difference where IQ falls short? The easy answer is that 90% of the workforce has an IQ between 110 and 120. IQ is primarily genetic. While it can increase throughout childhood and primary school, there is a predisposed limit on IQ. To set yourself apart in the workforce and to your peers, you need more than the 90th percentile.

For decades, the idea that high IQ and academic intelligence was the driving force behind success in the workforce. This widely accepted fact has slowly been losing its validity and being replaced with the idea that IQ is only part of the equation. In reality, IQ isn't even half of the equation! The division between the importance of EQ and IQ is not equal.

Take best friends, Henry and David, for example. They've known each other since they were five. They grew up next door to each other, played chess together, both swam on the swim team, and both got into top level technical institutes for college. Henry and David both have an IQ over the average. In fact, they have the same IQ of 167, off the charts smart.

Henry works for a large company as an IT support person, helping the other employees fix their computers, update their software, and work out any kinks. He lives alone in a one-bedroom apartment and despite going out every Friday night to bars, he doesn't usually meet anyone that he carries on long conversations with, or ever sees again. He hardly knows the other tenants in his building and most wouldn't recognize him on sight.

On the other hand, David is the CEO of a software development company that has an international market. He owns a large house in the suburbs with his successful, supermodel wife, and they are expecting their first child in three months. They host backyard barbeques with the neighbors and everyone in the neighborhood knows who they are and is part of their social circle. They invited over three hundred people to their wedding.

So, what happened to divide Henry and David's lifestyles so much? Based on their intelligence, education, and childhood experiences, they were both set up to have very successful careers. However, Henry lacked something that repeatedly inhibited his ability to get ahead or become successful. The only thing that Henry and David did not have in common in their young adult years was their EQs. While Henry greatly lacked EQ, David had a high EQ, leading his life in a much different direction.

Despite Henry's attempts at trying to rise through the company he worked for, he couldn't make enough of an impact with his intelligence alone. Sure, if there was a computer problem, everyone knew he was the best to handle it. But, if you ask any of the women how they felt when he came to their office to work on their computers, they would say that he made them uncomfortable. When pressed for details, they wouldn't report any kind of harassment or inappropriate behavior. They would simply say that he stared a little too long, or when he tried to talk to them, they couldn't understand him.

If you asked the men what they thought of Henry, they would most likely say he was brilliant, but they didn't like him personally. When asked for the details, there again, wouldn't be any specific inappropriateness or blatant reason. Mostly, they would report saying that it felt like he was trying to make them feel inferior for their lower IQ.

For these reasons, Henry was never noticed by management for possible promotions. In fact, this kind of "vibe" or "feeling" that other employees would talk about could have seriously hindered his chances of getting a promotion if he applied for a higher-ranking position. That social awkwardness, the inability to "read" his audience, and his ego centered around his own intelligence turned his peers off to wanting to get to know him personally. These are all signs of having a low EQ. Henry is clearly displaying a lack of emotional understanding in those around him and he can't adapt.

In his home life, this lack of EQ becomes even more evident. Most people that live in an apartment complex know some of their neighbors. Whether they just know their name and casually say "hello" when they run into each other in the hall, or if they actually socialize, it is common to know the neighbors. When Henry passes his neighbors, he will refuse to make eye contact and shuffle past. His low EQ prevents him from making that social connection with other people in casual passing. He can't interact with them because he doesn't know how to have casual interactions.

A person needs to understand body language and facial expressions in order to have casual interactions. As discussed in Chapter 1, facial expression and body language are quite often related to an emotional response or an emotional state. This aversion to contact makes Henry less noticeable to his neighbors and they are more likely to ignore him and his presence.

He lives alone because he has had repeated difficulty in forming personal and romantic relationships. Without understanding his own emotions, he hasn't been able to contribute properly to a relationship. With a low EQ, Henry hasn't been able to understand or navigate through his partner's emotions either. Therefore, when a partner goes through something emotional or attempts to connect to him emotionally, he doesn't understand. He can't be empathetic towards them and he can't be supportive in the way that a lot of people need their partners to be.

In the early months of a relationship, during the well-known "honeymoon" phase, these kinds of deeper emotional connections are overlooked. Henry is able to have a relationship that starts out great, but quickly devolves into a mess and a breakup. It isn't that he doesn't want to make it work or that he doesn't want companionship, he just has no way to achieve that goal because of his low EQ.

When Henry goes out on Friday nights to try and meet new people, he'll sit at a bar and usually wait for people to approach him. When a conversation is struck, it becomes obvious, fast, that Henry lacks social awareness. This leads to awkward silences, people getting offended and confused, and other people feeling like Henry is trying to make them appear dumb. He doesn't know when it is appropriate to tease or make a joke, and he might not even pick up on when someone is just teasing him. These emotion-based social interactions become frustrating and embarrassing for Henry and those involved.

Henry's low EQ repeatedly interferes with his ability to have any sort of normal or successful life. He isn't successful at work. He isn't successful in his romantic or social relationships. It all comes back to his low EQ. In Henry's case, his incredibly high IQ doesn't actually contribute to his chances of success.

David, on the other hand, has a high EQ and a high IQ. He rose through the ranks of a software company because of his relatability, friendliness, and the support he gave to his peers. Then he was able to develop his own highly beneficial software. Through his high EQ and charisma, he started his own company, took it international, and then met the love of his life.

Their relationship isn't perfect, because no romantic relationship is, but his EQ allows him to manage his emotions and navigate through hers. This led them to build a solid enough relationship to get married and start a family together. Their neighbors know who they are and love to have social gatherings like backyard cookouts and block parties. David isn't just successful in his career. He is successful in all the places where Henry isn't.

The differences that a high EQ can make in lifestyle, successes, and relationships are very notable between the contrasts of Henry and David's lives. David, as a CEO, is in a leadership position. EQ serves him very well in that leadership role. People with a low EQ who attempt to take on a leadership role can often end up failing or causing some large upset.

Imagine Henry, with what you know of his life, trying to be a manager to a team of primarily women. It seems unlikely that he would succeed where he makes them feel uncomfortable. Imagine him being the CEO of a company. How would he talk to shareholders, make business deals, or even talk to the company employees without offending them, making them uncomfortable, or misreading them? It is hard to imagine Henry being successful in any kind of leadership role.

It can happen. Sometimes people with moderate or low EQ's do get into a management position or leadership role. If you have ever worked a job where you felt the manager was absolutely unreasonable, impossible to relate to, and didn't seem to have the interests of their employees in mind, then you know what it is like to work under someone who has a low EQ. It is likely they didn't last long in the company, or when they finally had to leave, they probably weren't likely to find another management role.

It can be incredibly difficult to work with and under someone with a low EQ. Just the same as it is being in any kind of relationship with them, not just limited to romance. Fortunately, with the skills you are going to learn in Chapters 4 and 5, you are going to give yourself the ability to manage these interactions in a way that is comfortable for you.

Sure, you can't make your bad manager raise their EQ, but in raising yours, you'll know how to handle them better and won't be so frustrated or upset when working with them. Similarly, changing your EQ won't change that of a romantic partner or family member, but you'll gain the tools to interact with them in a way that alleviates the stress and tension for yourself, and probably them too.

The example of Henry and David's lives is a bit of an extreme. It was designed to point out the differences between IQ and EQ and to better illustrate why EQ is considered a larger contributor to success. Unfortunately, low EQ can also lead to other issues in someone's life. Not being able to establish relationships, being somewhat isolated socially, and feeling unsuccessful can lead to mental health problems like depression and anxiety, among others.

Now would be a good time to take a moment to analyze your own relationships. If you have failed romances, consider what it was that really went wrong. If you have had fallings out with friends or families, what contributed to those fallings out? Are there any past or present work relationships that you have which are difficult? Look at your coworkers, those that are peers, and those in management and leadership roles. If there are difficulties in these relationships, what are they? Where do they originate from?

By breaking down these conflicts, you can begin to see where and how your EQ has impacted your life. This can be difficult, because no one likes to admit if or when they were in the wrong. Be honest with yourself; that is how you are going to change yourself and make a difference in your own life. Do you relate more to David, or do you relate more to Henry from the anecdote? These two caricatures are incredibly exaggerated extremes. Most people fall in a more central zone with their EQ. Some people have great self-awareness but aren't able to manage their relationships or express empathy. Just like with IQ, there are many different places you can fall on the EQ scale.

Since emotional intelligence is multi-layered, where you fall on the spectrum could be closer to David than Henry, but still not up to the levels for the kind of success that David has achieved. You might find yourself closer to Henry, but not that low. Still, not having the EQ to rise out of the current success level you find yourself in. Regardless of where you find yourself on the emotional intelligence spectrum, the truth is, you can increase your EQ. There is hope!

Chapter 3:

Good News! You Can Improve

Your Emotional Intelligence

Since the notion that IQ is the primary factor of success has been losing popularity, there has been a lot more focus and study on emotional intelligence and how EQ promotes success. Unlike IQ, which is based on a genetic predisposition and levels off after a certain age, EQ has the potential to be changed and increased, even in adulthood. This makes it a more useful, versatile skill set.

A study published by Science Direct showed how emotional intelligence could be increased. This was a control-based experiment. Nineteen children were put into a group to be trained in EQ. These were four group training sessions that lasted two and a half hours, all in regard to emotional intelligence. The second group of 18 children continued to live normally (Nelis, et al, 2009, abstract).

The children that received emotional intelligence training showed a significant increase in their abilities to identify emotions and manage emotions. The control group showed no such changes. Additionally, the study group was followed up with six months later, and it showed that the results of the EQ training were still in effect, impacting the children's lives (Nelis, et al, 2009, abstract).

Of course, the study was also interested in seeing the improvement in mental health, physical health, performance in work and study, and also improved social relationships. All this was accomplished through this study. Do you know what that means? It means that educating yourself on emotional intelligence has the ability to make these changes for you too!

Increasing your emotional intelligence is about more than just setting yourself up for success. It is also about self-empowerment. By studying and practicing proven methods for increasing your EQ, you also gain something else that is likely lacking. You gain confidence, personal power and energy to put towards your goals. By taking responsibility for improvement, you give yourself something a lot of people lack. You give yourself control of where you and your life are headed.

The science is there to back up the goals behind what this text is offering you. You've seen research from reputable institutes that focus specifically on why EQ leads to greater success. If that isn't enough to get you excited about the proven strategies in the next two chapters, let's look at another example.

In this scenario, Cindy's longtime boyfriend of five years left her because he felt like they lacked a good emotional connection. Cindy would get stressed and aggravated about work and take it out on Mike. If she was sad or upset, she would shut down and ignore Mike. He felt like he was walking on eggshells around her, waiting for her to get angry, and then shut down and isolate herself. It was clear to Mike that neither he nor Cindy were happy.

In the aftermath of Mike leaving, Cindy spent a lot of time blaming him for leaving. She wanted it to be his fault. She told herself that he didn't understand her, that he didn't accept her. She convinced herself that Mike was weak and not the right man for her. She let herself believe that the reason their relationship ended was because Mike had some kind of emotional problem and couldn't commit, so he had to project his problems onto her.

She wanted to vent to someone all her frustration and thought about calling her mother or sister. Unfortunately, Cindy hadn't had a fluid relationship with her family in a long time. They were far away and every time she did see them, she felt like they were picking on her and berating her for one reason or another. As a result, Cindy had withdrawn. She communicated with them less and only saw them on holidays and important family events. She had no one to call and talk about her breakup with.

So, Cindy returned to her normal life and worked on getting over Mike. Several months later, an opportunity came up at work for Cindy to apply for a better job. She submitted her application, went through the interview, and was feeling really good about herself. A week later, she was told that the company had hired someone else for the role. When Cindy asked what it was that had gone wrong, she was told that her "people skills" weren't on the level that the company wanted for someone in that position.

Cindy's initial reaction was to be mad at her employers. She silently seethed, telling herself that she was an asset to the company and that they just didn't know all the work she did for them. She told herself that they didn't value her or her talents and wanted to hold her back from succeeding because they were worried she would outgrow them and leave. She seriously contemplated quitting her job to show them just how much they would need her once she was gone.

At the point where she was considering quitting, Cindy paused. She finally let herself look at the events of the past few months with honesty. She was able to admit to herself that she had been emotionally irrational and shut down, which is why Mike left her. She was also able to admit that she didn't have the greatest people skills at her job. The self-realization was hard and a little painful. Cindy didn't want to let it bring her down though.

Instead, she wanted to take action so that the next relationship she was in would succeed, and the next time she was presented with a promotion opportunity at work, she would get it! So, Cindy began to do some research and came across emotional intelligence. She took an EQ test and was a little surprised to find just how low her EQ was. She had hardly any self-awareness, little social awareness, even less ability to manage a relationship, and hardly any score when it came to self-management. Cindy knew what she had to do, she had to raise her EQ.

It can be very sobering to see results in black and white and read what each result means. There are several EQ tests out there, some paid and some free, that can help guide you in the right direction with your EQ. Knowing your scores is the first step in understanding what needs to be improved. You might be surprised to find which areas are higher or lower.

Alright, coming back to Cindy, she began a program of proven self-help strategies that would help her increase her EQ. She practiced mindfulness, began to strip away the negative and positive notions that surrounded emotions, and began to practice being in her own discomfort. The work was sometimes difficult and uncomfortable, but Cindy didn't want to give up. She was certain that she could succeed if she could make these adjustments in her life.

To help herself out even more, she sought the help of a professional that helped guide her through learning to empathize, putting herself in someone else's shoes, what to watch for in body language, and gave her tips for planning ahead with social engagements. She got feedback from the expert that was helping her and that opened up doors for more self-improvement for Cindy to initiate.

Through hard work and perseverance, Cindy was able to complete her program of increasing her EQ. She practiced the methods she was taught every day, over and over, until her brain naturally began to respond in the way she was training it to do so. She even began to notice some of the changes within herself, especially when her family members and friends commented on how different she seemed.

When she felt ready, Cindy retook the EQ test and was over the moon when she discovered that her scores had jumped up significantly. The next month, another opportunity arose in her company, and Cindy felt like she could apply for it. So, she did. To her complete joy, she was selected for the job. The interviewer and her manager made sure to tell her how they've noticed the improvement in her attitude and the changes in how she interacts with her coworkers.

In the end, it wasn't just the improvements that had made them think she was right for the job, it was her commitment to bettering herself. They'd been watching how her peers' opinions of her changed and had noticed Cindy becoming an almost completely different person in the workplace. They commended her hard work and were excited to offer her the promotion.

Cindy was so happy that she wanted to celebrate. Having spent time improving her relationship with her sister, Cindy called her up and gave her the good news. Her sister was excited for her and incredibly proud. It was one of the best conversations Cindy had had with a family member in a long time. Her sister lived a couple of hours away, and they made a date to get together for a sister weekend after Cindy got settled into her new job.

Still wanting to have her own celebration, Cindy reached out to her neighbor. While Cindy was working on her EQ she and her neighbor had connected and found they had a lot in common. It was a new friendship, but Cindy knew that this was a good time to promote the progression of that friendship. They planned to go out to dinner on Friday night to celebrate.

It was nothing fancy, but Cindy just wanted to have a good time. She and her neighbor made a reservation. They ordered a bottle of white wine, and they spent the evening talking about Cindy's new job, discussing her neighbor's impending engagement, and conversing back and forth about the kinds of things that friends indulge in. Even though the goal was to celebrate Cindy's victory at work, she didn't want the focus to be entirely on her and she kept including her neighbor so she wouldn't feel left out or bored.

As fate would have it, while they were out to dinner, Cindy and her neighbor ran into Mike! At first, Mike seemed a little reluctant to acknowledge them, but Cindy didn't confront the situation with shyness, awkwardness, or anger, as Mike would have expected.

Immediately, Mike could see a change in Cindy. She looked happier, lighter, and even a little more friendly. They struck up a casual conversation, as exes sometimes do, and she told him they were celebrating her recent promotion. Mike was impressed with the changes she had made in her life and even expressed pride at her getting that work promotion. By the end of their conversation, he was so enthralled with the "new" Cindy, that he told her they should go out for coffee sometime and catch up. Cindy agreed and then returned to her friend for the remainder of the evening.

A part of Cindy had wanted to invite Mike to join them for dinner, but she knew that could look disrespectful to her neighbor and maybe over-eager or over-zealous to Mike. She decided it would be best to set up a separate social engagement to interact with Mike, especially since they were only just reconnecting. Cindy didn't want to push or act too soon. She and her neighbor enjoyed the rest of their meal, and Cindy returned home with a great sense of pride and personal accomplishment.

Taking the initiative to change herself and increase her EQ gave Cindy several new opportunities. She got a promotion at work, made a new friend, and was able to reconnect with the partner she lost. Her successes went from almost non-existent, or completely unnoteworthy, to expansive!

In this anecdote, Cindy had enough self-awareness to realize that there was something about her that wasn't working in her personal and professional relationships. That self-awareness is difficult to find and admit to. However, since you are already reading a book on improving your EQ, then there is a part of you that knows there is something about you that can be changed in order to improve your success rates.

Can you think of times in your life where you think that having a low EQ made it difficult for you to accomplish something? Think about Cindy's reactions in the first part of the story, how defensive and angry she got. Can you relate to the feelings and thoughts she had when something in her life didn't go the way she had planned? Now look at her successes by the end of the story. Is that the kind of change you want to make in your life? Are those the kinds of personal goals you want to accomplish?

Regardless of what your personal success goals that you are looking to achieve are, working on your EQ is going to set you apart and give you a much greater insight into yourself and how to let all your dreams unfold. Cindy put in a lot of work to raise her EQ and change how she related to and interacted with other people. Beyond that, the rest took care of itself!

When you move into Chapter 4 and 5, you will really begin to see what is involved in increasing your EQ. You will learn proven methods and strategies that teach you about mindfulness, empathy, walking in someone else's shoes, being in your own discomfort, removing the negative and positive associations from emotions, what to watch for in body language, and how to plan ahead for social engagements.

This list of skills is a small portion of what you will learn in the next two chapters. In Chapter 4, the focus will be on self-awareness and self-management. In Chapter 5, you will move onto social-awareness and managing relationships. As previously illustrated, the four concepts of emotional intelligence all build off of each other. Regardless of where you currently are on the EQ spectrum, it is best to start from the ground and work your way up.

Cindy had a lower self-awareness, and that made it even more difficult for her to manage relationships, empathize, engage socially, or manage herself. However, improving one aspect doesn't automatically improve the others. It is a collective process that continues to build on itself until your entire brain chemistry is essentially altered.

During the process of increasing your EQ, it is very likely that people will notice the changes. Just like with Cindy, you'll get feedback. People might comment on your mood or attitude being different. They might tell you that you appear more social or relaxed around other people. If you have a spouse, family, or long-time partner, they will probably see changes in you too. The feedback from these people is important and can be the encouragement that you need to continue through your transformation.

While the people closest to you take notice of the progress that you make, there is a very high chance that your relationships with these people will begin to improve as well. You'll be able to have a more positive relationship with your family, and repair any damage that has been done over the years. You'll be able to reconnect with friends and strengthen those bonds to build a support network with them. In your job, you'll be able to foster closer relationships with your coworkers and your superiors in the office. You might even begin to feel like part of the team.

If you have a partner or spouse, you'll probably begin to notice that handling arguments, miscommunications, and misunderstandings becomes much easier. In being able to regulate your own emotions, but also being able to read their body language and emotions, you have the potential to diffuse situations or manage them in a way where both you and your partner are satisfied with the conclusion.

As much as people like to think otherwise, romantic relationships do take work and effort. No relationship is perfect and that is because every person is an individual. When you have a long-term companion or live with someone long term, the tension and potential for loss can be a lot greater. Maybe that is why it is so easy to have detrimental arguments, there is so much more at stake. Either way, EQ is your path to maintaining a healthy, stable, and strong romantic relationship.

It is worth mentioning that improving yourself is hard work. You'll be starting with self-awareness, and this is often an area that individuals struggle with most. Looking at your own flaws or where you have a lower score for EQ isn't very fun. Most people avoid self-reflection because they know they won't like what they see. You might already suspect that you aren't going to like what you find, why else would you be reading a self-help book?

Be gentle with yourself. People with a low EQ have generally not been taught the skills required for proper socialization, interaction, and emotional management. Like most skills, they have to be taught, learned and practiced. If you never had the proper education, that is hardly your fault. So, remember that, despite what you've lacked in the past, you are now taking the initiative to change your future.

You should also be aware that raising your EQ does take a commitment on your end. It is not an overnight process that instantly fixes everything. It takes work and it takes time. There will be times when it seems frustrating or hard to stick to your goals. Having the expectation that this is an involved process will hopefully help reduce that frustration when it arises.

You will have to be dedicated to the practices. It is up to you to practice and repeat those strategies that are given to you. Your brain can relearn how to think and how to react, but it needs to be a conscious effort that is full of repetition. Just reading the methods isn't enough. You have to make them a part of your everyday life. You have to make them a part of yourself.

Make the promise to yourself now that you won't give up. That you are devoted to raising your EQ and choosing a better, more successful future for yourself. Tell yourself this, believe it, and now, put it into practice!

Chapter 4:

Proven Strategies to Improve Your Self-Awareness and Self-Management

Strategies for Improving Self-Awareness

Since your emotions manifest quicker than rational thoughts, if you aren't aware of them and how you respond to them, your emotions end up controlling you. This isn't always a bad thing. However, if your emotional responses cause discord in your life, then awareness is the first step to bringing them back under your own control. What are some uncontrolled emotional responses?

Explosive anger is a common, extreme emotional response. When people think of uncontrolled emotions, anger is usually the first to come to mind. It isn't the only one though. Grief and sadness can become overwhelming and detrimental leading to depression and an individual's inability to move on with their own life. Even an emotion that is as enjoyable as happiness can result in extreme emotional responses. You may have met, or been, someone who has a very intense joy. That happiness can be so intense that it unnerves people around them and makes them uncomfortable.

Being aware of how your emotions manifest and how they impact you and the people around you is the first step to being self-aware. The following methods and strategies are going to help you increase your own self-awareness to boost your EQ.

Stop Labeling Emotions as Good or Bad

One of the stigmas that surrounds emotions is that there are good emotions and that there are bad emotions. This is untrue. All emotions have evolved as part of who and what humans are from thousands of years ago. Every emotion has a purpose within society and for social interactions. Your emotions can even help you to pick up on danger and assist your survival skills.

While it may not seem like you need to know about dangerous situations on a regular basis, the fact of the matter is, your emotions have a purpose. It is that purpose that you are going to need to better understand. In the meantime, it is important to begin to establish a healthy relationship with your emotions, all of them.

Some of the emotions that have the strongest stigmas and are the most criticized internally and externally are anger and grief. A lot of cultures see anger as a negative emotion that should be suppressed. We've already discussed why suppressing and bottling up emotions doesn't work.

Grief is another emotion that gets a lot of negativity. There are gender biases surrounding grief, indicating that men who feel or express grief are somehow weak or less masculine. If someone doesn't recover from grief in an "acceptable" amount of time, their peers, coworkers, friends, and family members can begin to be unsupportive and start to persecute said griever for not "getting over it."

While you'll never be able to control what other people do, you can start by letting go of these preconceived notions of good and bad emotions. All emotions are necessary. None are better or worse than any others. Liberate yourself from such limiting and harmful thoughts about some emotions being good and some being bad.

This is one of the first, and one of the hardest changes, you'll need to make towards self-awareness. When you attach "good" and "bad" labels to your emotions, your mind will subconsciously resist the "bad" emotions. This might be in avoidance, denial, or other methods of trying to protect yourself from bad emotions. Unfortunately, that kind of enforced "protection" doesn't result in eradicating the "bad" emotions from your body chemistry.

Empower yourself by making your emotions your ally. It takes a lot of work to remind yourself every day that your emotions aren't good or bad. To remind yourself that your emotions are a part of who you are and are necessary. Emotions developed as part of human evolution, that means each emotion you experience has something to tell you.

If it helps, put a sticky note on your front door, refrigerator, mirror, or another place you will see it every day. Write a reminder for yourself that emotions aren't good or bad. Putting this in your mind every day will help you to release the stigmas that surround emotions and give you the ability to begin listening to what your emotions are trying to tell you. When you acknowledge that all your emotions are important and necessary, your mind won't default to suppression, avoidance, or denial and then you can get your emotions working for you, not the other way around.

Train Yourself to Be in the Discomfort

More often than not, emotions will manifest physically in the body. If you are feeling anxious, your muscles might tense up and your palms can get sweaty. If you're happy, you will smile, maybe even laugh. Sadness can result in heavy breathing and tears. This is how your emotions communicate with you. They manipulate responses in your body to tell you exactly what you are feeling.

A lot of times, these physical manifestations can cause varying levels of discomfort, especially when you are in public settings. Even when you are alone or in limited company, you might have a strong emotional reaction that makes you feel uncomfortable. Where does this discomfort come from? Well, a large portion comes from the social and cultural associations with emotions. Due to these associations, people learn from a young age what society views as "acceptable" and "unacceptable" for emotions.

Depending on the family you grow up in, there could even be familial associations that were imposed on you and your emotions. Discomfort in what you feel usually stems from shame or some other "negative" implication. After you are able to accept and truly believe that emotions are neither good nor bad, you can allow yourself to feel the emotion as it manifests in your body.

Even if the result is uncomfortable, you want to experience it, without any prejudices if possible. As you really feel what your body is going through, you can start to associate these specific responses with the emotions that trigger them. It is true that everyone feels their emotions differently, but there are some core physical responses that have been observed by researchers to be experienced almost universally when it came to the six core emotions from chapter one.

So, by identifying your body's reactions as they relate to specific emotions, you can start to understand what your emotions are trying to tell you. You can also use this as a way to become aware of what emotions you are feeling and what is the trigger or source of that emotional response. It takes practice to work through your emotions and how they manifest physically.

Remember That Bad Moods Are Temporary

Bad moods come and go. It might seem like common knowledge, but it is important to remember on your self-awareness journey. Sometimes you just have a bad mood, and you can't always determine a reason.

You could drive yourself crazy trying to come up with reasons as to why you are having a bad mood.

Moods are complicated and often not directly linked to any one event or experience. An anniversary date can put you in a certain mood, someone's birthday, a dream you had the night before, a plot twist in a book you're reading or show you are watching that was unexpected. When a bad mood comes up, it is usually the result of a culmination of events or feelings that have reached their breaking point.

Have you ever had a bad mood that makes it difficult for you to focus on your work? Maybe it makes you angry at your spouse or children. These bad moods can create a significant amount of unrest in your life, even though the mood itself is fleeting. You can say or do things under the influence of a bad mood than can be hurtful to others or create friction for you with peers and coworkers. These reactions aren't necessarily something you really feel, but when a bad mood strikes, it can take over your entire day!

The important thing to remember with bad moods is that, whatever the reason, it already happened. As you go through your day, try to remind yourself that the people you see and interact with aren't the cause of your mood. It can help you to limit any unnecessary emotional reactions that can be harmful to you or others.

The good news is, bad moods aren't stagnant. They come and go. This is another acknowledgement that will help you maintain some kind of emotional control during a bad mood. Since emotions aren't rational, you have to consciously tell yourself to use logic when it comes to bad moods. Learning to separate your thoughts and your actions from a bad mood is incredibly difficult work. It takes time for your mind to be able to make that distinction.

However, once you master the deviation between a bad mood and your logical thoughts and actions, you can experience a bad mood without it influencing your entire day. Bad moods are temporary. Knowing that and understanding that will help you create the separation between a down and out mood with your ability to move through your daily activities without your mood being an influential factor.

Pay Attention to How Your Emotions Are Affecting Others

Once you are aware of your emotions and how you respond to them, another important step to self-awareness is in finding out how your emotions affect others. This will continue to be part of your EQ growth, especially with social awareness and managing relationships. For now, you'll want to start out a bit smaller. If you can't accurately tell how someone else reacts to your emotional responses, ask them.

This method, of course, might not work well with complete strangers and casual interactions. However, with friends, family, coworkers, and a spouse or partner, you can ask them their opinion on what your reactions make them feel or how your reactions affect them.

This exercise isn't meant to be disruptive to your relationships, so you'll want to find a time that isn't in the middle of a heated argument or upsetting conversation to approach the subject. However, if these people in your life are aware of your quest to improve your EQ, then they might be anticipating these kinds of questions and the need to provide feedback. Before you really get started, you can let people in your life know that this is a plan of yours and suss out who is willing to give you constructive feedback so you can change yourself.

You might be surprised by how willing people in your life are to help out when you've made the commitment to this kind of change. That being said, don't force the matter with anyone who is uncomfortable or resistant to the idea.

When you inquire into how your emotional interactions impact others, it is important that you remain open to the feedback. To be honest, you probably won't like all the feedback you get. Even so, you might find it beneficial to take some notes on the feedback people give you so you can have reference points when you begin the practices and strategies for social awareness.

Knowing how you affect others isn't just an aspect of social awareness, it is also an aspect of self-awareness. This is self-awareness, being cognizant of your impact on others.

Get Curious and Find Out What and Who Gets Your Emotions Going

Before you can move on from improving your own self-awareness, you are first going to have to recognize what makes you feel a specific way. Basically, you are going to be analyzing your emotional triggers. When you're aware of what brings on certain emotions and certain responses, you can then prepare for situations based on this knowledge and awareness.

Below there is a table that you can use to help you break apart emotional reactions to get to the core of why you responded a specific way. This is a tool for reflection. After any event or situation, refer back to this table and answer all of the questions.

Event	Feelings	Negative Thoughts
What was the source? What happened? Where were you? Who was involved?	Which feelings did you experience?	What was I thinking? Why am I thinking this?

Starting with the event or situation, you'll want to break it down into exactly what happened, who was involved, and where you were for the event. By breaking it apart you can see if there were any pieces that you can off the bat identify as a trigger or someone or something that contributed to your emotional reaction.

If you can't, that's okay. That is why it is a three-step process. At this point in your self-awareness journey, you should be familiar with your emotions and what you were feeling based on your personal responses and reactions. So, take the time to pick apart what emotions you felt during this event or situation.

You'll also want to analyze your thought patterns. You'll want to consider how your thoughts differ when they are fueled by emotion versus when they are based in logic. One of your goals with raising your EQ is to train your mind to act rationally before reacting emotionally, despite its innate programming to act the opposite. If you can reflect back on what your thoughts were at the time of an emotional event, then you can take a moment to think about how it could have played out differently if rationality had come into play.

Picking apart your emotions and their responses isn't always easy after the fact. The mind likes to try to compensate and make excuses. That is why it is important to overcome the mindset of good and bad emotions as well as opening yourself up to feedback and criticism before you get to this point. You want to be able to reflect back as honestly as possible. Only then will you be able to identify your triggers. Preparing yourself for situations where you know you will encounter an emotional trigger is one step towards increasing your EQ.

With enough time and practice, you won't need as much prior preparation. Your mind will naturally default to a logical reaction instead of an emotional response.

Keep an Emotional Journal

A great tool that can be used for personal reflection, observation, and objective review is keeping an emotional journal. You should take some time every day to write in your own journal specifically about your emotions and your emotional responses. This is another reflection tool that can help you identify triggers, name emotions, and know how you react in response to certain emotions. Take note of not only your emotions but your physical responses too. It will help you better relate specific reactions back to specific emotions.

Through taking notes on what you experience, you'll have an easier time understanding what emotions and triggers bring you down. You'll also be able to determine what emotions and triggers lift your moods up. You'll be able to identify exact triggers in the form of people, events, situations, and other details that may escape you when just trying to think back without a reference point.

Through writing, you'll achieve a better way to reflect back. Since self-reflection can be the most difficult type of personal growth, having it in black and white, written on paper, you'll be able to get a better sense of your strengths and weaknesses. Especially when it comes to your own emotional awareness and your emotional triggers.

You can use your journal to ask, and answer, the question, "How much do my emotions affect my normal routine?" This is an important question because you want to be able to see the differences in how your daily life changes as you get a better handle on self-awareness and your emotions.

You can reflect back on your own writing to determine how your moods impact your decision making and your thought processes. Since you will be working towards separating your emotional and rational responses, understanding when and how your moods affect your other processes is going to be key in making that separation.

This emotional journal is also going to be a good place for you to take notes on the feedback you get when you ask them how your emotional reactions affect them. If you write down exactly what they say, then you can look back and see what responses triggered reactions in people around you. This awareness can help you uncover your own emotional triggers as well.

Another aspect of self-awareness that is going to help you, and ties into asking for feedback, is writing down the feelings you have when you are confronted. Even if the confrontation is instigated by you, in regard to asking for feedback, you'll still want to be aware of how it makes you feel. Having things written down, whether it is in an actual paper journal, a simple notebook, or even if you keep a digital journal, not only will you have a tool to reflect back on so you can improve your EQ, but you'll also have a way to track your own progress.

Seeing how much you've changed or improved over time is a huge motivator for you to keep going.

Evaluate How Well You Are Living up to Your Values

When it comes to self-awareness and being honest with yourself, you are going to have to take a look at your values and beliefs. These are important, because they are going to be directly linked to your goals for success. Since everyone is different, your goals and aspirations are likely different from what other people hope to achieve by raising their EQ. Use the table below to write down some of the core beliefs and values you have as well as how they relate to your goals.

Core values and beliefs	Anything I've said or done recently that goes against my values and beliefs
• • • •	• • • •

Once you have those values and beliefs written down, move to the second column in the table and consider anything you've said or done recently that doesn't align with your beliefs and values. Here, you will really be able to see how emotions impact your thoughts and actions in an irrational way.

Your core values and beliefs are going to be based on logic and rationality. They coincide with your wants and goals. Yet, when you look at thoughts and actions that don't align with them, you'll be looking at emotional responses that were produced without rational thought.

Seeing the differences presented on your table, or the contradictions that manifest between logic and emotion, you will have a deeper awareness of the impact your emotions have on your life and your inability to reach your own goals. Start small with this tool, sticking to core beliefs and values. Remake the table again and write down your goals and desires, then compare what you have been saying and doing that contradicts what you want.

The more you review these contradictions, the more you'll be able to see what is holding you back emotionally. You'll have a list of thoughts and actions that can be traced back to previously analyzed emotions and emotional triggers. This tool will help you break away from the thoughts and actions that prevent you from getting to your goals. Having that ability increases your self-awareness and boosts your EQ just a little more. All of these tools and skills are going to help you as you move into self-management, social-awareness, and hanging relationships.

Seek Feedback

Just like learning how your emotional responses affect others, you should reach out to your friends, coworkers, family members, and other people close to you for feedback. In order for this to work, you'll have to be open to feedback and accepting of what might be said or learned.

Since you have already been reflecting on yourself and been honest with your own shortcomings as well as what you need to improve in yourself, you should be more open to receiving feedback.

When you ask for feedback, you'll want it to be as specific as possible. You'll want to know the details because when you write them in your journal, you'll use those details to compare similarities. These similarities in feedback are going to give you inspiration to keep going and also find areas that still need improvement. There is a big difference between how you see yourself and how other people see you. While it is true that you can't be responsible for how other people react to you, you can still take responsibility for how your reactions impact other people.

That responsibility comes in the form of empathy. Your awareness will help with that empathy. You'll be able to practice shifting the way you react around certain people based on their feedback. This is one of the first steps in learning how to interpret other people's emotions. It is a good idea to take notes based on feedback in an organized way that also lets you review who gave you what feedback. This will come in handy later when you begin analyzing other people's body language.

Having a high EQ is also about knowing when and how you can change your own behavior to impact those around you. The feedback you get will serve as a starting point for you. In the beginning, it will help you track your own progress and give you insight into where you need to put more effort. You'll want to reflect on the feedback to note how it changes over time. You might be surprised to find just how other people's perceptions of you change as you increase your own self-awareness.

So, even as you work on yourself and your self-awareness, you are preparing to extend these skills and knowledge towards the people you interact with. You are well on your way to make a difference in your EQ score.

Make an Effort to Understand Yourself Under Stress

Stress is a natural, common emotion that is experienced and felt by everyone. Most people don't go a single day without feeling some form of stress and/or anxiety. Stress is a survival emotion. When your body experiences stress it is really trying to tell you something. The physical manifestations of stress can be mild or extreme.

There can be a loss of focus, tense muscles, irritability. More extreme symptoms of stress include insomnia, loss of appetite, physical illness, and in very severe cases hair loss or weight gain. Stress can literally cripple the body if it isn't addressed. Since stress can manifest as so many symptoms, and since a lot of cultures and society strive to create stressful environments, stress is often overlooked as a root cause of these symptoms.

Since stress is a common emotion, one that has potentially debilitating effects, it is a good idea to identify what you experience as stress. Understand your body during stress and leading up to particularly stressful situations.

With your journal, begin to compile a list of traits and responses that you recognize as stress and then take a step back and start to identify the events and situations leading up to those stressful overloads.

Being aware of what comes before stress and how the stress presents itself will help you get ahead of your own stress. Managing stress can be incredibly difficult and sometimes time-consuming. This is especially true for people who don't know what causes their stress, can't admit they are stressed, or are perpetually stressed and don't even know it.

Have you ever lashed out at someone for something small and insignificant because they happened to be in the wrong place at the wrong time? That is probably your stress coming out. Have you ever been on the receiving end of a stress response from someone else, where you felt their reaction was unjust to your contribution? That is most likely their stress manifesting.

Since stress can trigger emotional responses that are over exaggerated, intense, and usually result in irritability and lashing out, you want to know about your own stress as you grow towards the goal of increasing your EQ. As you learn the signals and signs of your own stress building, you'll want to begin practicing stress management techniques. This will help you to default to stress relief rather than build up and lashing out.

Stress relief techniques will be elaborated on in more detail in future sections. However, there are a few you can begin practicing when you discover your stress build ups. Taking deep, slow breaths with your eyes closed can help your entire body and mind relax away from stress. Counting up to 10 in a very slow, methodical way can also bring your stress levels down significantly. If you find that you are particularly prone to stress, you might even want to try meditation or drinking chamomile tea to help bring yourself back to a relaxed state before you get sent over the stressful edge.

Strategies for Improving Self-Management

You may already be feeling more comfortable and self-aware just by reading through the previous sections. You'll still want to practice those strategies every day until they become like second nature. Even while you are working on your self-awareness, you can also begin to work on your self-management as well.

This section of the book is going to focus on not just being aware of your emotions when you reflect back on them, but also knowing what you are feeling as you feel it and how to manage your reactions and interactions.

Practical Strategies

Challenge Your Thoughts

Event	Feelings	Negative Thoughts	Alternative Thoughts	Results
•	•			•
•	•	•	•	•
		•	•	

When you challenge your thoughts, the goal is to discover what thoughts of yours trigger extreme emotional reactions. Just like with external stimuli, internal stimuli, in the form of thoughts, can also trigger emotional responses. Thinking about a specific memory or event can trigger emotions. Also, having thoughts about yourself or other people can trigger emotional responses. Self-deprecating thoughts are particularly good triggering unwanted emotions.

Using the table above, begin to challenge your own thoughts when you have an event or situation that causes an unwanted emotional response. Begin by recording the specific event. Add onto that the feelings you experienced as a result of that event. Then write down any negative thoughts you had about yourself, the other people involved, or the situation as a whole as a result of those emotions.

You'll have to have a decent grasp on self-awareness to complete this table. The next box, jot down a few alternative thoughts that you could have had that weren't negative. After reviewing the non-negative thoughts, consider how you feel differently about that event. Take note of this in the "results" column.

Practicing this kind of thought management takes time and practice. Try to use this table at least once a day to help yourself better understand how your thoughts can influence your emotions. Over time, you will be able to identify the kinds of thoughts you want to be having so that you reduce the negativity associated with events and emotions. This table can demonstrate how intricately connected thoughts and emotions are. If you are able to manage the thoughts that your mind associates with certain emotions, then you can literally change how your emotions impact you and the people around you.

This is an important exercise in self-management. It is a bit more involved and long term than some of the other methods in this section. However, if you practice it a little every day, you will begin to see the changes in yourself when it comes to what kinds of thoughts your emotions produce.

Practice Deep Breathing

One of the symptoms of stress that was discussed at the end of the previous section was shallow breaths. Shallow breathing inhibits the function of the brain. Oxygen doesn't get circulated properly. Have you ever noticed a near lightheaded feeling you get when hyperventilating? That is because oxygen is being inhaled and exhaled too quickly for the body to process. Thus, the brain doesn't get the oxygen it needs to process thoughts and think rationally.

This kind of shallow breathing leads to a lower brain function and is not optimal for managing yourself and your emotions. Poor breathing in general can have long term effects on the body and mind. This is why deep breathing is such an integral part of many Easter philosophies. Yoga, Tai Chi, meditation, all these practices incorporate a breathing aspect that is designed to energize, revitalize, and rejuvenate the body and mind. A lot of these breathing practices have been used for thousands of years, and have been used to combat stress.

Through self-awareness, you are going to be discovering your stress triggers. However, by teaching yourself to breathe deeply automatically, you can actually limit the amount of stress that your body feels. The beauty of this practice is that you don't even need to feel stressed to practice it. If you can, try to set aside ten minutes a day to practice deep breathing.

Sit or stand with your spine straight and your chest open. Take a deep, slow inhale in while mentally counting up to four. Hold that breath in your lungs to the count of four. When you exhale, do so slowly and deeply all the way to the mental count of eight. Repeat this breathing pattern for those ten minutes.

Not only is this deep breathing exercise designed to help you breathe better and reduce stress, but it also helps the body expel old, stale air from the lung sacs. Next time you feel yourself building up stress, take a seat and practice this deep breathing. You'll physically be able to feel the stress draining from your body.

Count to 10 With Slow Breaths Between the Numbers

Another deep breathing exercise that helps with stress reduction and management is counting to 10 while taking deep breaths in between each number. The goal for this exercise is to give your rational mind space to exist separately from your emotions. It also serves as a tool to empty your mind of thoughts that are influenced by your emotions. Then your logical mind can step in.

Have you ever heard the advice, "If you're feeling angry, count to 10?" It is a common tool to use in stress, anger, and other intensely emotional situations. However, adding the deep breaths is what gives this exercise a leg up over just counting slowly to ten. It gets that vital air moving through your system and moves oxygen to your brain for healthier function.

So, you begin this exercise by saying mentally or verbally the number one. Follow that with a deep, slow inhale and a heavy, slow exhale. Then move onto the number two. Repeat this counting sequence with a deep breath in between numbers all the way up to 10. Once you reach 10, follow with another deep breath. You might find it beneficial to close your eyes when you do this. Removing visual stimuli can help your thoughts and emotions relax further into those breaths.

One of the benefits of using this breathing technique, especially when you are angry, upset, or stressed, is that it engages your rational mind and thoughts. Your emotions get sent backstage so they can't run the show anymore. This is a good exercise to use if you know your stress is building or if you encounter any of your emotional triggers. Before you even have a chance to react, close your eyes and begin the breathing sequence.

Not only does it help you out of a potentially uncomfortable and explosive situation, but it helps to teach your mind that rational thought should take precedence over emotional reactions. Through practice and perseverance, your brain will be retrained to respond that way.

Be Humble and Seek Out an Expert or Someone You Know Who Seems to be Really Good at Handling Their Emotions

During your self-realization journey, it is a good idea to seek out the assistance of a professional, an expert, or someone in your life that you know is good at managing their own emotions. A professional could be someone who has written about emotional intelligence, someone who has studied emotions and psychology and applies this in their work, or even a therapist who has been trained in mindfulness and emotional intelligence.

An expert doesn't necessarily have to be professionally involved in a field of study with emotions, but may be someone you know who studied psychology in college. Maybe someone you know who has researched the topic of emotions and emotional health either for their own gain or to help someone they are close to.

There are most likely people in your life that are already good at managing their own emotions. You've seen it when interacting with them. It might even be more obvious to you now that you know what you've learned through this book.

Whichever avenue you decide to take, make a connection with someone that is knowledgeable on the subject of emotional intelligence either through daily application of research. This person can be your main source of feedback and encouragement. They can also help by pointing you in the right direction.

Start by meeting with them once a week to discuss emotional intelligence and what you have been doing to improve yours. You might want to focus specifically on self-management and what they do or suggest for regulating emotions. The methods that can be used span a wide range and there are as many methods as there are people. You'll have to find what works best for you.

Having someone help with ideas and suggestions is going to make coming up with management practices a lot easier for you. After you meet with them, take time to reflect on what you discussed and what you learned. After a month, stretch those meetings out to every two weeks. This will give you additional time to reflect and practice, but also put enough space between meetings that they will be able to give you feedback in regard to changes they notice between visits.

Prioritize Time for Problem-Solving

Decision making is directly influenced by your emotions. You make decisions a thousand times a day, even without realizing it. The clothes you wear, what you eat for meals, if you work out in the morning, whether or not you decide to read the paper or listen to the news, what time you leave the house to go to work; these are all decisions you might make in the first ten to twenty minutes of you waking up and getting out of bed.

A lot of decisions happen subconsciously because of a routine you've established or because they aren't life altering, they are almost automatic. There are decisions that you'll be faced with that can pose a larger impact on your life. Some are much more impactful than others, like taking a shortcut to get home from work faster versus accepting a job three states away. A lot of decisions have to be made on the spot in the moment, but there are some that you have time to make.

Now, it is common knowledge that hastily made decisions are rarely effective or beneficial. While a certain amount of spontaneity can be fun, it should generally be reserved for fun. The important decisions should be approached with rationality. For example, when a relationship is ended in the heat of the moment during an angry argument, one or both parties often feel regret and remorse after the fact and will try to fix the relationship. However, if the time is taken to analyze what is wrong and if/how it can be fixed, then a more reasonable compromise or conclusion can be reached.

Set aside 20 minutes of time for yourself every day to do some problem-solving. Your emotional journal is a good place for this work. You might want to write down some impending decisions you have coming your way. Weigh the pros and cons, consider different angles and outcomes for whatever you decide. Get yourself in the habit of analyzing these decisions so that you are less likely to make them based on intense emotions and irrational thoughts.

Take Control of Your Self-Talk

In the same way that self-deprecating thoughts can manifest from emotions, negative self-talk can also be a result of your emotions. Negative self-talk would be any kind of words or phrases that you use against yourself. When you insult yourself, belittle yourself, and depreciate yourself, you are using negative self-talk, even if it is a mental monologue.

You'll want to take control of this self-talk. While self-talk stems from emotions that produce negative thoughts, remember that thoughts don't necessarily reflect reality. Although thoughts are very real, they are often biased by the thinker's opinions and emotions. In this case, your opinions and emotions are influencing the negative things you say to and about yourself.

Start to look at what emotions and thoughts trigger negative self-talk for you. When you isolate the causes, think of what kinds of things you could say to and about yourself that aren't negative, but still reflect on the trigger you experience. While these alternatives don't necessarily have to be overly positive and bursting with happiness, think of how you can take away the negativity and replace them with neutral or positive statements instead.

Any time you speak negatively about yourself, get in the habit of taking a step back and considering a better alternative. When you have that alternative, repeat it to yourself a few times, mentally or aloud. This will help rewire your thought patterns towards the positive self-talk and replace negative. Having confidence is one part of emotional intelligence that helps with social interactions and meeting your success goals. Confidence is built on a positive image and opinion of yourself.

So, by managing the thoughts you have about yourself, you are able to improve your own opinion of yourself. This will later lead to a buildup of confidence. If you look at the people around you who are successful in their careers and relationships, they will show confidence in all their interactions. They hardly second guess themselves, even as they remain open to alternative opinions. Being confident doesn't mean thinking you're always right or always the best, it just means that you are comfortable with yourself, your beliefs and convictions, and that will stand out.

Make an Effort to Cut Off the Worst of Your Negative Emotions

Negative thoughts about yourself and about the people around you, as well as about your job, your relationships, etc. begin to weigh heavily on your emotions and your ability to create your own success. Negativity is like a magnet that you carry in your pocket. Every time you have a negative thought it gets stuck to that magnet, making the magnet heavier and heavier. It gets harder for you to move through your day with that negativity dragging you down. Of course, this creates a vicious circle of feeling even more negative.

Since emotions are neither good nor bad, negative nor positive, it is the thoughts, opinions, and biases that you have which are contributing to the heavy magnet you are lugging around. It is a sobering, and hard to accept thought, to realize that we are all our own worst enemies and the one thing that is usually holding us back is, well, us. But, in knowing that, you have the ability to pull that negative magnet from your pocket and get rid of it!

The practice of reframing your thoughts so that they don't default to negativity is hard and time-consuming, but the payoff is entirely worth it. Did you know that you can literally reshape your situations and experiences simply by refraining from negative thoughts? It is entirely possible to shape your own reality, but you need to see it with light and positivity if you want to create a positive reality.

A good way to get started is to focus on small victories. If you were able to make it to work on time every day for a week, acknowledge that and celebrate it. Maybe you were able to make it to your kid's soccer game one evening when you normally couldn't. That is a small accomplishment, but you should own it and feel victorious. Give yourself room to appreciate the little achievements that you make. This will help you to find positivity in all situations, big and small. That is what you should be celebrating, and over time, your mind will automatically seek that positivity, making you feel great about all kinds of situations and events!

Create a Healthy Sleep Environment

Sleep is crucial to human survival. It is also vital to emotion management as well as rational thought, cognitive function, and maintaining energy levels. Unfortunately, modern society seems to shun the needs for sleep as well as use devices and tools which quite literally prevent the body from getting a restful sleep.

Coffee, soda, and caffeinated beverages are a major staple in a lot of a lot of modern cultures. Caffeine has an unusually long half-life though, it takes a long time to break down in your system. Drinking coffee after noon means that a significant amount of this stimulant will still be in your system by eight or nine o'clock at night. A good rule of thumb is not to drink caffeinated beverages after noontime.

Smart phones, tablets, televisions, and laptops all have screens that give off blue light. This blue light inhibits the melatonin production in the brain, a chemical needed for sleep, by tricking the brain into thinking the sun is still up. A good practice is to turn off all electronics for about two hours, but no less than a half hour, before going to bed. You shouldn't sleep with your phone or devices near or in your bed, unless you can put them on airplane mode or turn them off entirely.

Working or watching television in bed is going to impair your mind's ability to turn off and rest. Even reading in bed can keep the mind stimulated. It is best to reserve your bed for sleep and sex only. This will help your mind get in the habit of relaxing for sleep when you lie down. Blocking unnatural light sources, such as windows where headlights reflect, is also a good idea.

You should establish a regular sleep pattern as well, going to bed at a specific time and waking up at a specific time. This is going to make a huge difference in your body's ability to maintain healthy sleep patterns.

Speak to Someone Not Emotionally Invested

Another good way to get honest feedback is to find someone you know who will talk to you honestly and give you feedback, but who isn't too close.

People who are personally and emotionally invested might rely on their own biases. This could lead them to believe things that aren't true about you, see progress because they want to see it, or the opposite.

They won't mean to give you unreliable information or observations, but emotions have a way of getting in the way.

If you can find a coworker, or an acquaintance, maybe the spouse of a friend that you see somewhat regularly but don't know really well, who is willing to give you feedback, then you are in good shape. This person should know who you are, at least on the surface. Friends, family, spouses and partners tend to be too emotionally close to you and that will compromise their observations and feedback.

You want to take care of who you choose. They should be someone that you trust and who will expand your horizons. You want to know that they will be honest, and even though they don't have an emotional stake, you'll want them to be constructive rather than critical. Harsh criticism can cause setbacks in your progress. Speaking to someone who understands how to give feedback without being downright cruel is the best way to go.

Avoid choosing someone who you know will agree with everything you say. This method is meant to give you additional perspectives. If you speak to someone who agrees with everything you say, then you'll limit your own self growth and you won't ever move beyond your current boundaries or thought processes. You can set yourself up to succeed by choosing the right person for this process.

Schedule for an Emotional Unload

Physical activity is a fantastic way to release emotions. Not only does the brain secrete a lot of beneficial chemicals when you exercise, but it has other benefits. Your body remains healthier, it contributes to establishing a regular sleep pattern, helps regulate moods, keeps your energy levels and ability to focus up, keeps you alert, as well as helps with making you an effective planner, with organization, and with decision making.

Try to get at least 20 minutes of activity a day to be an emotional unloading for you. It helps to flush emotional baggage and make room for the beneficial process. Remember, this activity doesn't have to be a rigorous, sweaty workout. You could go for a twenty-minute walk in a park, do a yoga routine, run on a treadmill, play with your dog, there are a lot of options that range between extreme and mild.

There are other ways that you can unload emotions that aren't directly linked to physical activity. Getting regular massages, one every four to six weeks, will help to release emotional baggage and junk. You could even look into other kinds of body work which rely on energy movement such as Reiki, Polarity, acupuncture, and reflexology.

Being outside in nature with yourself, or your dog companion, and listening to natural sounds can be incredibly soothing and therapeutic for releasing emotions. Maybe you'll just sit on a porch swing and read a book on a sunny afternoon. Lying out in the sun, as long as you keep yourself protected with sunblock, is another great way to unload emotions.

This kind of emotional unloading can be called self-care, or personal time. The goal is to get the brain producing serotonin and dopamine, as well as to expose yourself to Vitamin D, which you get from the sun. With these three chemicals, you keep your moods up and help remove emotional junk from your body that contributes to heavy, negative feelings.

Make Yourself More Resilient

Mindfulness

Mindfulness is a type of meditation practice that teaches you to be in the moment. It helps you to work towards not letting your thoughts and emotions control you. Mindfulness practices can be simple or complex. Practicing mindfulness every day is a great way to help you separate yourself from your emotions and your thoughts. It is another method that takes consistent time and practice for results. However, since there are simple mindfulness practices that only take minutes, working them into your everyday life can be quite easy.

A simple and non time-consuming mindfulness practice is to eat an orange (or any kind of fruit). While you are eating your orange, close your eyes and focus on the complexity of what you are tasting. Keep your attention on the way the juice and the fruity flesh feels in your mouth. Think about what it smells like, and what you taste and feel as you swallow, following that feeling all the way down to your stomach. With each bite, analyze the sensations you experience.

This simple mindfulness practice slows down the process of an everyday task, such as eating. It pulls you away from the rest of the world and all other distractions, keeping you focused on exactly what you are doing and experiencing as you are experiencing it. There are phone apps that you can use, two well-known apps are "Calm" and "Headspace." Both of these are apps that offer mindfulness exercises that you can use for your own improvement.

In the past few years, research on mindfulness and how it can help against depression and anxiety has skyrocketed. A lot of people are taking an interest in mindfulness as a way to regulate thoughts and emotions. There are even mindfulness therapies that are becoming commonly used in the cognitive-behavioral field (McCarney, et al, 2012, abstract).

Practice Delayed Gratification

Delayed gratification is the opposite of instant gratification. Human minds, bodies, and emotions are programmed towards wanting instant gratification. What exactly is instant gratification? Well, it is when you do something that gives you an immediate feeling of pleasure, happiness, or joy. You don't have to wait for any sort of "payout." It happens instantly.

Unfortunately, there are a lot of bad habit forming methods for instant gratification. Some of the most commonly abused sources of instant gratification are cigarettes, alcohol, sugar, and caffeine.

What is the point of practicing delayed gratification? This strategy towards making yourself resilient and being able to manage yourself ties into impulse control. Impulses are powerful urges to do something, an almost physical need, to act irrationally and hastily. Have you ever heard of impulse purchasing? That is when you buy something that you really want the moment you see it, without considering things like your financial status, if you'll ever use the item, or what you gain from the purchase. A lot of impulse buys come with buyer's remorse and regret after the fact.

So, teaching yourself impulse control by practicing delayed gratification is going to help you manage your emotions and thoughts better. Especially in more extreme situations.

Some exercises for practicing delayed gratification could be cutting sugar out of your diet for seven days. If you drink a glass of wine with dinner every night or have a couple of beers after work, spend a week without alcohol and remove that "feel good" amenity for a while.

If neither alcohol nor sugar feature prominently in your daily life, consider taking a cold shower. Complete your washing routine, spending at least five minutes on it, or longer. Then, transition to a warm shower, slowly as not to shock your nervous system, but only allow yourself two to three minutes in the warmth before ending your shower.

These are willpower practices that help you to manage your own thoughts and emotions over time. You might even choose this time to quit smoking cigarettes. You'll already be practicing other methods for stress reduction and managing yourself. It might be a good time to quit a bad habit, like cigarettes, without the stressful side effects.

Chapter 5:

Proven Strategies to Improve Your Social Awareness and Relationship Management

Strategies for Improving Social Awareness

Step Into Their Shoes

One of the most fundamental practices of social awareness is imagining what it would feel like to be in the other person's shoes. It sounds like a grade school cliché, but the truth is, one of the best ways to relate to someone else is to take a look at a situation through their eyes, from their perspective.

When you interact with other people, there should be a regular question in your mind. That question should be, "How would I feel if I was in their situation?" This question can be in regard to any personal problems they are dealing with or even how they react to something you say or do.

Stepping into someone else's shoes is also a good way to reflect on your own behaviors. If you have an interaction with someone that doesn't go as you had planned or hoped, think back to what happened and ask yourself, "How would I have reacted if our roles were reversed?" Regardless of what was said or done, imagine how you would have felt or reacted had you been on the receiving end of what you said or did to that other person.

You can learn a lot about yourself, but also about human interaction in general by experiencing situations from both sides. It is hard sometimes, to imagine what someone else is thinking or feeling. Therefore, you can put yourself in that position and envision how you would think or feel. While it might not be the same as what someone else experiences, it is usually enough to form a compassionate and empathetic response.

So, while you start stepping into other people's shoes, you get to look at events and interactions from multiple perspectives. You begin to develop your empathy, and you might even notice that your opinions of certain people begin to change. If you try to step into someone else's shoes and your immediate response is, "I can't even imagine," then you should realize that there is no reason for you to be making judgments about that person.

Use this tool as a way to reflect on how you can change your behavior, but also use it to help you understand the reactions and responses of other people.

Take People's Past Into Account

A person's past is hugely influential to their emotions, thoughts, and behaviors. A lot of these aspects are learned from parents, teachers, siblings, caregivers, family members, and through culture. Sometimes, these habits and behaviors are developed as a form of survival and self-preservation, with the goal of fitting into a social group unnoticed.

It is important to remember that everyone has a past. This same past is going to contribute to an individual's ability to communicate, interact, and understand other people. When you are interacting with other people, keep in mind that their past is a large influence to how they act and respond. Whether you know the details of their past or not, it isn't for you to judge these behaviors.

Rather, ask yourself a couple of questions. First of all, ask yourself, "What needs does that person fulfill by using that behavior?" The answer might not be obvious, but if you think about it, or even think about why you would behave in that same way, you might be able to gain some insight into their behaviors. When you understand someone, you can step away from frustration and judgment, feeling compassionate and empathetic instead.

The second question you should ask yourself is, "What could have happened in the past to explain this behavior?" You might never get the answer to that question. Other people's pasts are their own and they are under no obligation to share. Asking this question is a direct reminder that behavior and emotional responses comes from a lifetime of experiences.

When you are able to see other people as having experiences that have shaped and molded them, and when you've considered what experiences have made these behaviors and what the behaviors are used for, you'll find yourself feeling less frustrated. Interacting with people becomes easier as your levels of empathy increase. As you understand other people's behaviors better, you can adjust your own behavior so that it helps to meet their needs. Having that insight and ability to make changes to accommodate them is a huge leap in EQ.

Greet People by Name

It is an unfortunate fact, but in the age of technology where the majority of interaction is happening through cell phones, text messages, and social media, the art and courtesy of greeting other people by name has begun to diminish. This is a fantastic emotional intelligence and social awareness tool.

It is incredibly basic, therefore easy to practice. It is a great way to establish rapport and break the ice. Greeting someone by name makes the interaction more personal. It makes the person on the receiving end feel happy, they are seen and acknowledged as an individual. It personalizes the conversation or contact by making them a featured topic in your mind. They will feel important to you.

The tactic of greeting people by name creates a warm and open atmosphere for the interaction to take place. It can also help to break down barriers and make the person you are communicating with less defensive. Have you ever spoken to someone closed off and defensive? It can be hard to have a smooth conversation as they might question everything you say, and even their body language can become hostile.

While a name isn't the answer to everything, when you include a person's name in your greeting, it automatically creates a sense of comfort and familiarity. Someone who might not even realize they are being defensive, will have an easier time relaxing into that familiarity.

If you are meeting someone for the first time, greeting them by using their name is a great way to establish a connection that can easily become trust. In a work environment, using people's names in casual passing or in work meetings makes them feel less like a cog in the machine. They become an individual. It is almost like you return an aspect of their personal identity to them.

Since so much social interaction happens impersonally these days, it is easy for people to feel unseen behind a screen or through a phone line. Using their name makes them seen and gives them their own identity again. Try it the next time you go out to your favorite coffee shop or restaurant. Look at nametags and greet whoever waits on you by using their name. You might be surprised by how many warm smiles you get and how different the interaction feels. The next time you see friends or family, use their names with a personal hello to each one. This will create a deeper intimacy between you and the people you are already close with.

Watch Body Language

Body language is often a physical representation of what someone is thinking or feeling. As you learn about the way your own thoughts and emotions manifest in your body, you should start to watch other people's body language too.

When watching for body language, what is it you should be watching for? The most obvious is going to be body posture and physical gestures. These movements are often larger as they use the entire body or a whole limb. There are more subtle movements and gestures you should also be looking out for.

Watching the face for facial expressions is a part of observing body language. It is more than just looking at the mouth for frowns and smiles though. Thoughts and emotions can show up around the mouth, through movements in the nose, cheeks, eyebrows, and forehead. Sometimes these expressions are minute and isolated, other times they take up the whole face.

Even subtler still, watching the way someone's eyes move can be a very good indicator of what they are thinking or feeling. This is also true in people who are incredibly controlled and might not be as emotive or expressive through their face or body. Eye movements can indicate fear, sadness, anger, anxiety, boredom, stress, happiness, comfort, and a whole range of other emotions.

When you are interacting with someone, make a conscious effort to observe their posture, gestures, facial expressions, and eye movements. Try and figure out what they are trying to tell you, what you are hearing without verbal confirmation. If you are unsure, try asking someone you are comfortable with what they are thinking or feeling when they make a certain gesture or expression.

If you observe animals in the wild, most of their communication is nonverbal. A twitch of the ear, crouching low to the ground, lifting a tail in the air, or raising hackles; these are all types of animal body language. Believe it or not, modern humans in history evolved without a spoken language. They relied on those body language cues for communication. The body is evolutionarily programmed to respond to thoughts and emotions. There is a lot of communication that happens silently. Tapping into that hidden line of communication will give you a great advantage in understanding and interacting with others.

Like greeting people with a name, understanding body language is becoming a lost talent. However, it is vital to proper and effective communication between humans.

Understand the Importance of Timing

Communication and social awareness is about more than just reading body language and understanding other people. Once you practice those skills, what do you do with them next? Well, you learn how to use them in order to have successful interactions and give yourself an advantage to reach your goals. But how do you do that?

One way to utilize what you've learned is to practice and understand the importance of proper timing. For example, if you have a question or favor for someone, you want to make sure they are in a mood or mindset to be receptive. If you ask someone a favor while they are angry or sad, you probably won't get the response that you hoped for. If you wait until that person is in a happier or calmer mood, you're more likely to receive the answer you hoped for.

You want to gauge the other person's mood before bringing up certain topics, waiting for the right time to ask certain questions or have certain conversations. Is it the best time to talk about marriage with your partner right after the two of you have a huge argument? Probably not.

Timing is about more than just understanding the other person's mood. You'll also want to consider recent events. If your friend just lost their dog, asking them to accompany you to the vet with your dog is a little insensitive, even if they seem to be coping with the loss. Granted, you can't always know what is happening in someone else's life. Additionally, when you are at work, it is almost expected that personal issues are left outside the workplace so that the focus can be on getting work done. Still, through reading body language, you'll be able to tell who is approachable and who is closed off.

If you aren't sure about the right time, default back to the practice of stepping into someone else's shoes. If you have a favor to ask someone but they seem upset, and you aren't sure if being asked a favor will make them more upset, take a step back and think about how you would feel being asked a favor when you are upset. You can combine certain skills that you have been practicing to help you get a better grasp on appropriate timing.

This extends beyond just asking questions and favors though. You'll want to make sure that you bring up topics, jokes, and even teasing other people at the right times. A misplaced joke, or teasing someone when they aren't receptive, or bringing up a conversation topic that your audience isn't open to can result in a social disaster. Read your room in order to help understand the best timing.

Plan Ahead for Social Arrangements

Prior to going to a social event or engagement, take a moment to consider who else will be attending. With all the progress you've already made in self-awareness, self-management, and social awareness, you'll be able to establish a sort of baseline for the crowd you will be a part of.

It might help to come up with some conversation topics that you know will be well received by that particular crowd. For example, going to a dinner party at a vegetarian's household, you probably don't want to plan to talk about the pig roast wedding you attended the previous weekend.

Planning ahead for your social arrangements ties back into timing as well as reading your audience. Instead of doing so in the moment, you are going to do a little prep so that you are more comfortable going into the situation. It isn't a bad idea to have a few tricks up your sleeve, especially if you still have any lingering anxiety about social gatherings.

It is important to remember, that regardless of the prep work you do, you'll still have to be cognizant of other people's moods and mindsets. It is still important to read body language and you might need to adapt your plan in the moment if things aren't as you anticipated. Don't let that stress you out, just think back to all the skills you've been practicing and you will be able to make adjustments as needed.

Generally, the idea of planning ahead gives you the ability to focus on the people you are with in the moment, rather than being anxious about what you will say or do. This is related to mindfulness practices. By having preplanned topics of conversation, you can focus more on observing body language as well as listening to the people you are interacting with. By being fully present with them your interaction becomes more genuine and deeper.

Be Mindful of Your Contact

When you are having a conversation with someone, or if you are in a work meeting or a class lecture of some kind, it is a social awareness skill to be really listening to what the other person is saying. You don't want your mind to be wandering to what you are making for dinner that night, or when your next doctor's appointment is.

First off, it is a little rude to be thinking of other things while you are engaging in a conversation. Second of all, your thoughts manifest physically just like your emotions. Especially if your thoughts trigger an emotional response. You might subconsciously display body language that indicates you are feeling a certain way which the person speaking can pick up on. They won't understand your reaction to their words and it could take the conversation in an unexpected turn.

More than that, if your mind is wandering and the speaker picks up on that, they will be able to tell that you aren't focused, that you are bored with the conversation, or that you aren't interested in what they have to say. This creates a hostile atmosphere where you've demoted the speaker to be less important than whatever is happening internally in your thoughts.

Part of social awareness is learning how to have positive interactions with people. To practice focusing on the speaker, enter into a conversation or meeting or social interaction with the intention of learning something based on what the other person says. This way, your mind will be focused on listening to them so you can learn something new.

If you happen to catch yourself not paying attention, immediately stop your train of thought. Take a deep breath and refocus your attention on the speaker. You might even want to lean towards them a little bit so your body and mind know to focus on the words being said. Mindfulness exercises are a great way to help practice focusing on a single task or person without your mind wandering off.

Practice Active Listening

Listening to what is being said, comprehending it, and learning something new is only half of what listening is all about. Active listening is the skill in which you listen to the tone the speaker is using, you listen to their volume, the speed at which they are talking, and to any fluctuations.

This kind of listening is similar to watching body language. The way someone talks is going to give you additional clues into what they are thinking and feeling. Tone, volume, and speed are lost through electronic communications. This is another reason that so many people don't know how to use active listening or know how to listen to tone, speed, and volume.

When someone else is talking, focus entirely on them. You should be listening to what they say, how they say it, and their body language. Together, these three outward signals are going to tell you everything you need to know about what the other person is thinking or feeling.

Proper active listening isn't just about focusing on the subtleties of the voice, but it is also about being an active participant in the listening. Just like with the previous section, someone else can tell if your mind is wandering. To stick to the active listening model, position yourself so you are facing the person that is speaking. Make eye contact. Don't stare the other person down, but use that eye contact to show you are focused on them and what they are saying.

During pauses in the conversation, nod to reinforce that you are listening, or insert small words of encouragement like "yup," "uh-huh," "no way," and other situationally appropriate words and phrases that indicate you are not just listening, but that you are understanding what is being said. Practice not interrupting. Sometimes it can be difficult to tell when someone finishes a sentence or a thought. Listen for longer pauses and watch for signals that they are waiting for a response or that they've finished their current thought.

These are all components of active listening and how to make a social interaction flow smoothly. They are skills that take practice to learn, understand, and master. You might find it helpful to practice having a five to 10-minute conversation with someone every day so you can improve your active listening skills.

Learn About the Culture

Now, after all your study, practice, and progress, it is time to introduce a bit of a curveball. This curveball is different cultural expectations. Not all cultures have the same body language, facial expressions, or behaviors to coincide with what you've come to understand as acceptable in your own culture. Some cultures have clothing that covers parts of the face, making it more difficult to determine facial expressions.

If you don't have the opportunity to make observations about certain cultural interactions before you end up in a situation where you are interacting with people of another culture, don't panic! Revert back to observing those subconscious body language indicators. Humans all evolved in similar hunter-gatherer circumstances. Therefore, the instinctive emotional responses and physiological reactions are very similar across the board.

If you can get a grasp on those fundamental biological reactions, then you'll have a better time interacting without accidentally offending the other person. Another option too is to ask if a certain behavior or gesture is acceptable. Asking might seem blunt, but in reality, people from all over the world will feel a sense of gratitude if you make the effort to learn about what is appropriate for them culturally. It can create a sense of comfort, because it shows them that you care about making them feel at ease.

There might be events or situations where you have time beforehand to do some research on cultural norms for other cultures. While some research can definitely break the ice, asking directly might be better received. If you go into a situation acting like you already know about their culture, that can be seen as offensive. So, do some preliminary research just to have a starting point, but don't be afraid to ask specific questions about appropriate behavior and body language.

There are so many instances in which you might come across other cultures. The business world is expanding internationally across many different countries. Refugees are moving around looking for safe havens for their families, and there is a lot more international travel now than there used to be. The more you practice with other cultures, the more you will be able to apply those same skills to interactions with people of your own culture as well.

Ask to Test Your Conclusion

Sometimes, the best way to make sure you are interpreting someone's body language correctly is to just ask. It sounds almost too simple to work, doesn't it? Well, there is a tactful way to ask about someone else's mood that won't come off as blunt or insensitive.

For example, if someone looks upset, going up to them and saying, "Wow, you look really upset, what happened to you," isn't the best approach to getting a beneficial answer. Nor is it a sensitive or empathetic way to approach someone else's emotions. Instead, try phrasing the question more like, "It looks like you're feeling a little down, did something happen?"

A properly phrased question opens up the potential for honest communication without making the other person feel ridiculed or like they are being judged. Not only will you get a response that helps you to better understand what someone else is thinking and feeling, but you will also improve your communication skills by practicing the right phrasing of questions.

These two exercises together will increase your empathy. It will also help others to see you as someone they can turn to for support because you pick up on subtle moods and emotions. That is a huge step in increasing your EQ and is going to go a long way as you begin working on managing your relationships in the next section.

When in doubt, ask. You might even want to write down some pre-thought out phrases or questions in your emotional journal. Have a few different questions written out for different scenarios that involve different emotions. If you think you need help coming up with tactful, empathetic questions, ask someone else who is good at talking to other people and expressing empathy. They can help you come up with appropriate questions to ask.

Practicing asking these kinds of questions is also a good way to improve your own social awareness. Just like with timing and active listening, there is a way to ask and phrase questions and comments so that they are better received.

Seek 360-Degree Feedback

Now that you have come a long way through self-awareness, self-management, and social awareness, it is time to start getting more in-depth feedback from more obscure sources.

Rather than relying on people you know and trust for feedback, expand your network outward. Begin asking coworkers, your boss, students you attend classes with, even consider asking your clients and customers. These people have likely noticed changes in you as you strive to raise your EQ. Some might even come out and say it.

However, it isn't a bad idea to ask for some kind of feedback. With clients and customers, maybe you can write up a kind of survey that they can choose to fill out at the end of their interaction with you. Include some feedback questions about the interaction so you can get some insight into what they think about you and how you handled the interaction.

Having a survey like that is sometimes a good way to get the most honest feedback because people are apt to be more honest on paper, especially if it is anonymous. They won't attempt to say what you want to hear instead of what they actually think.

Feedback is going to be the primary reflection tool that will allow you to grow and raise your EQ. Self-reflection is great for admitting you need improvement, but in order to track that improvement in a way that reflects how you are impacting the people around you, you'll need feedback from the person you are interacting with.

Sometimes, even after all your exercises and the skills you've practiced, a behavior you have defaulted to that is meant to be helpful is actually unhelpful or offensive to many people. This can tie right back into asking questions and using the appropriate phrasing. It isn't enough to want to be helpful when someone is upset, you have to develop the right tools to be helpful when someone is upset. This is where empathy is going to play a major role.

The feedback you get from people you interact with, but who aren't close to you, is going to show you how empathetic you are being and where you still need to put effort into improving.

Strategies for Relationship Management

Despite what popular culture might have you believe, all relationships take time and effort. There is an initial "honeymoon" phase when the chemical secretions that create the feelings of love and joy are at their highest. During that time, all relationships seem perfect. The truth is, no relationship is perfect, regardless of how long a couple has been together or how flawless they appear. Everyone is different, and those differences can sometimes cause friction, arguments, and disagreements.

With the skills you've learned about self-awareness as well as self-management, and social awareness, combined with the skills you are about to learn, you can manage your relationships better. The differences between you and your partner or spouse won't cause lasting problems or explosive arguments due to this grasp on management.

Be Open and Be Curious

Being open towards other people is a great way to give them enough information so they can feel like they understand your perspective. It can be hard to be open and let people in. The concept of being open doesn't mean divulging your darkest secrets every time you meet someone for the first time. Rather, it means don't hide yourself. Let your partner see a softer side of you, be honest about your thoughts, opinions, and feelings.

A basic example of this kind of situation could be that you value punctuality. If someone is even five minutes late to a date, gathering, or meeting, it irritates you. The importance of being on time stems from several years of service in the military. If you are to share that you value punctuality because it was ingrained in you for years, rather than jumping to irritation when people show up late, you give your partner a reason for why you appreciate them being on time.

Now, the truth is, not everyone will understand your reasons for expecting timeliness from the people in your life, including your significant other. If they don't understand or are unwilling to compromise, then the pairing might not be a good fit for other reasons. At least, by opening up and telling them about your military past, you give them the opportunity to understand and change their behavior out of respect for you.

Along with openness, you should express curiosity towards your significant other as you want to understand their reactions and behaviors. Not only is this a good way to get to know someone, but the two of you should establish early on what kinds of quirks and pet peeves you both possess. Respectful couples will accommodate these seemingly "small" personality traits in their partner. It isn't about "changing" for the other person, it is about respecting that they are different from you and that you value them enough to make adjustments in your behavior towards them to show that value. Ideally, they will be willing to do the same for you.

Being open and being curious is a give and take process for you and your significant other. You both should practice revealing something little about yourselves every day, especially in the beginning when everything still feels new and blissful.

Try Not to Give Mixed Signals

Everyone is familiar with the concept of mixed signals. What is a mixed signal though? When broken down, a mixed signal is essentially when you say one thing, but your body language and facial expressions say something else. Remember when the importance of body language and nonverbal communication was discussed? Well, here is a very good reason as to why body language is important.

If your body language is closed off and your facial expressions are hostile, but you are speaking in a happy, light tone, then the person that is listening to you is going to be incredibly confused. Mixed signals are often seen among couples when they argue. One might try to pretend not to be as upset as they are and try to blow off the concerns of their partner, but their body language responds to their emotions and not their words.

When you give your partner a mixed signal, it leads to more than just confusion. It can create a larger problem on top of whatever the current issue is. If something upsets you, or you are offended, or don't have the time to do a favor, be honest about it. If you try to hide it, you'll end up contradicting yourself through your body language.

A lot of people aren't used to asking for help or are constantly functioning on a stressed out level. Their natural response to someone asking if they need help is to say something along the lines of, "I'm fine, I can do it," even as their body language shows that they are incredibly stressed and overwhelmed.

If you receive a mixed signal from your partner, recognize that it is likely the result of a learned behavior and not an attempt to be spiteful. When you encounter a situation like that, rather than asking if they need help or if they are okay, ask if there is anything they want you to do. Asking for a more specific answer, rather than one they can easily blow off, will get a more genuine response and be less likely to result in a mixed signal.

Practice not giving mixed signals. How do you do that? Well, this is a good time to fall back on your body language observation skills. Take note of the body language that you express in certain situations where you know that the words you are saying don't line up with what you are feeling. If you ever catch yourself doing that, stop, apologize to your partner for the conflicting messages, and be honest.

Be Open to Feedback

Allow your partner to give you feedback about their opinions and views of you and your reactions. Getting feedback can often be uncomfortable and make you feel self-conscious. Go into this process acknowledging that it isn't going to be easy to hear everything that your partner or spouse has to say.

Ask for specific examples about what you've said or done and use active listening to really focus on what they are saying. It is a defense mechanism to tune out topics that make you uncomfortable. This is a natural human reaction. So, when asking for feedback, be prepared to refocus your attention on what is being said so that you can understand fully.

Regardless of whether or not you agree with the feedback that you've gotten, thank your partner or spouse for their honesty. You want them to feel like they can share their perspective with you. You want to be receptive of the feedback they have. You won't entirely understand how you need to adjust your behaviors in regard to your relationship unless you can understand the effect you have on the other person.

Keep notes in your emotional journal about the feedback you receive. Use those notes to make a plan on how you can use the skills you've learned to make adjustments in specific aspects of your relationship to improve the opinions and perspectives your significant other has of you.

It is worth noting that you can work on yourself and make a lot of changes in regard to your own EQ to improve relationships. However, you can't be responsible for what your partner is willing or unwilling to change about themselves. Even if you are putting a lot of effort into your own growth, if they have a low EQ and are unwilling to take responsibility for raising it, a relationship still might not work. Raising your EQ isn't a miracle fix to relationships. It certainly helps, but a relationship is a joint effort, and you can only do so much on your end.

That being said, direct feedback from the person that you are trying to improve your relationship with is going to be entirely worth your time and effort as you work towards bettering your skills with managing your relationship.

Try an Open Door Policy

In the workplace, an "open door policy" refers to your superiors being open and available for you to come to with any problems or concerns. You can have this same sort of policy in your relationships as well.

An open door policy doesn't mean that you are constantly available for everyone whenever they need you. Rather, the idea of an open door for your relationships is being as available as possible but still understanding and setting the expectation that you can't be everything to everyone all the time.

One of the greatest downfalls of relationships in this current day and age is that people expect their spouse or significant other to fill all their emotional needs by being constantly available, supportive, and understanding. Unfortunately, it is impossible to be everything for everyone. That is why individuals should have strong networks of friends, family, and coworkers outside of their relationships. That way, you have a support system that doesn't include your partner and the other people in your life can help fill certain emotional needs your partner can't, or shouldn't be expected to.

This unrealistic expectation of your partner or spouse being everything you need emotionally is a huge reason why relationships fail. Having a high EQ helps you understand that you need to have multiple support systems and be able to manage your own emotions without expecting someone else to do it.

That being said, you still want to establish a policy that shows your partner or spouse that you are there for them. It is important for you to be supportive, emotionally available, and able to contribute to your relationship, but it is also important for both of you to maintain your independence and individuality.

You might find it helpful to observe how other people utilize an open door policy in their own relationships and then find out the best way to make one work for you. Communicate with your significant other when and how you can be available for them emotionally and how you can support them. When they know what to expect, they will be less likely to place unrealistic expectations on you.

Even so, there is a certain amount of emotional support, time investment, and being available that is required for a relationship to work. Otherwise, there is no foundation for the relationship beyond the initial attraction, and that isn't enough to hold a relationship together.

Get Mad When It Makes Sense

As previously mentioned, anger isn't a bad emotion. It has its purposes in society and in social interactions. Even if you are head over heels in love with someone, there is a good chance that they will make you angry at some point. The goal behind relationship management isn't to avoid anger at your partner or suppress it. It is about figuring out how and when to use it, and when and where to manage it.

This step is going to take a lot of practice and work. Anger is one of the most impulsive emotions that people can experience. Start by opening your journal up again and using the skills you developed through self-awareness to figure out what it is that makes you angry.

Be as specific as possible through this process. Write down triggers, events, people, words, phrases, and any other details that contribute to your anger. You should also write down the specifics of what your thoughts are in response to anger as well as your physiological responses and your behavioral responses.

Next, fall back on your social awareness skills to observe and write down how your partner or spouse reacts to you when you are angry. Write down what you observe in their body language, what they say, how they say it, and other behaviors that come out in response to your anger. Be as specific and detailed as possible with this reflection.

It isn't easy to be this honest with yourself about how your actions impact someone you care about. Relationship management is about honesty though; honesty with yourself and your partner. It is also about making choices in regard to yourself and your significant other that will help form a deep emotional connection.

This honesty means admitting that there will be times that you are going to get angry. Now, instead of letting that anger become impulsive and take control of the situation, a true test to your raised EQ is learning to use that anger in a way that benefits the situation somehow. You want your partner to know if they do or say something that angers you or upsets you. That doesn't mean that you scream in their face or punch walls over it. You can express your anger to get your point across without it becoming explosive.

For example, let's say the two of you just got a puppy and you are potty training your dog. Your partner finds a pee puddle on the floor and shoves your puppy's nose in it in an attempt to shame the dog for peeing in the house. You see this and recognize it as a harmful punishment for the dog and an antiquated training technique which makes you mad because you think the puppy might be emotionally scarred.

Rather than jumping all over the situation with an angry outburst of shouting or declaring that your partner is abusing the puppy or doesn't know how to train the dog, let the initial moment pass. Then, when you are calmer, let your partner know that you don't agree with that method of training and that you consider it abusive to the animal. You can show that you are angry about it, but keep it at a simmer. Don't just leave it at that though, offer to show them the appropriate way to potty train the puppy so that they learn something.

Don't ignore your anger, just make it work for you instead.

Do Not Avoid Events or Persons

Avoidance is a defense mechanism to protect yourself from being in a situation that you think will make you uncomfortable. Unfortunately, avoidance is also crippling to EQ. The only way to become comfortable in a situation or with another person is to face that discomfort and work through whatever is making you uncomfortable.

That was one of the first steps when working on self-awareness, being in your discomfort. To prevent anxiety over an interaction that you would rather avoid, first identity for yourself why this particular situation or person makes you anxious. When you know the truth behind the source, you can set boundaries for yourself.

Boundaries are important to EQ and emotional wellbeing. Boundaries refer to preset, metaphorical lines that you won't allow people to cross. For example, if you have a friend or parent that always teases you about a certain memory that makes you uncomfortable, set the boundary for yourself that if they bring that memory up, you will let them know that you don't appreciate that joke. You might also set a boundary for yourself that if they bring it up, you'll end the interaction early and separate yourself from the situation.

If you are setting a boundary for yourself in regard to another person, you might want to tell them about the boundary prior to the interaction so they understand what line they can't cross. Giving them the boundary prior to the event or interaction means they won't be blindsided by your reaction. By giving them your boundary, the ball is then in their court. They can either choose to respect your wishes, or they can test your resolve.

Boundaries are important for you to set so that you can go into situations that you would rather avoid with a sense of protection and an exit strategy. Establishing your own boundaries is going to give you a thicker skin that you can put on whenever you are required to interact with someone or go to an event you want to avoid.

When setting boundaries, be mindful that they should be beneficial to both you and the people you are interacting with. You shouldn't set impossible boundaries with unrealistic expectations that set yourself, or someone else, up for failure. It is also important to stick to your boundaries or no one will respect them in the future.

Acknowledge Other People's Feelings

A hard lesson to learn is that you can't control other people's emotions. As humans, it is common to want to control everything around us. This need for control originates from the desire for certainty. Humans want certainty. Control provides certainty. The truth is, you can only control yourself, your own actions, and your own emotions and thoughts.

Letting go of the desire to control other people's emotions is going to make a huge difference in your life and your relationships. One good practice to implement is to acknowledge other people's feelings. By acknowledging them you aren't agreeing with them. This method isn't to change what you think and feel so that it aligns with what other people think and feel.

Acknowledging other people's emotions validates what they are feeling and gives them the sense that you care, that they've been heard by you. A simple acknowledgement could be saying something like, "I can't imagine how hard that must be," or "It makes me happy to see you so happy." These phrases validate what someone else is feeling and it makes you a part of their emotion without making you responsible for it.

You can also use questions to acknowledge the feelings of someone else. A question for acknowledgement might be, "You seem upset, is something bothering you," or "Is there anything I can do to help you through this?" You want to show your support, show your empathy, even if you can't relate specifically or agree with what the other person is feeling.

It is a common problem in relationships when one person thinks their partner doesn't understand or empathize with them simply because they don't agree with how they feel. People wouldn't be individuals if they didn't have opposing opinions and feelings though. Support doesn't mean that you agree with their feelings, it just means that you acknowledge them and are willing to offer aid when they need it.

Build Empathy and Compassion

There have been a lot of inclinations hinting at empathy and compassion being necessary to improve EQ. So, here it is, skills and methods to increase your empathy and compassion. Several of these methods have been talked about in previous sections for different reasons, but they still lend a hand in building empathy and compassion.

Looking at situations from someone else's perspective is always going to help you establish more empathy and compassion. Even if just for a moment, you can separate yourself from any biases and consider how other people are affected by your actions and behaviors. You can step into someone else's shoes in many situations, not just ones that are about interactions you are a part of.

If a group of your friends is judging or belittling someone else and you are inclined to join in, think about how you would feel to be on the receiving end of that. You can develop compassion and empathy for people you aren't directly interacting with based on how others interact with them.

Another piece to look at with empathy and compassion is the values and beliefs of others. This doesn't specifically relate to religious beliefs, but religion can play a role. With friends, coworkers, and acquaintances, you are less likely to know about their personal beliefs and values. Ask yourself if it is possible that the people you interact with have different beliefs or values than you, and if that could be why you two don't see eye to eye.

Couples don't need to share beliefs and values to have a workable relationship. People of different spiritual, religious, and ethical backgrounds can make a relationship work simply through empathy and compassion, as well as respect towards their partner's beliefs and values.

Remember that everyone comes from a different background, which will contribute to their reactions and behaviors. Their own beliefs and values might even contribute to their stress and tension levels, which should be a consideration of yours.

Another piece of empathy and compassion is acknowledging that the reason behind someone's feelings and behaviors is probably related to something else entirely than whatever they are reacting to. This ties back into the notion that everyone has a past. Those past experiences create responses and behaviors. You should be of the mindset that there is probably a reason someone is behaving and reacting a specific way, a reason that developed in their past.

Keeping these three key points in mind, you will open yourself up to be empathetic and compassionate to the people you interact with.

When You Value Someone, Don't Be Afraid to Show It

In romantic relationships, but even with friends and family, it is important to remind people that they are valued. This doesn't have to be a big, extravagant expression with gifts and doting and praise.

Don't shy away from letting other people know that you value them. A simple expression could be sending a text message to your significant other, reminding them that you love them. Maybe you'll send your mother a card on her birthday thanking her for everything she's done for you.

It could even be less subtle than that. Say your wife spent all day cleaning the house and then made a big dinner. Give her a kiss on the cheek and thank her for her hard work. Or, simply thank your spouse or significant other any time you notice the effort they put in. These little reminders that you value them are going to strengthen the emotional bonds that you share.

This is true of your friends and family as well. Even your coworkers. After a work meeting, maybe you'll reach out to whoever ran it and say that you can tell how much effort they put into the presentation. Valuing other people isn't just about putting a smile on their face though. Although, it is always nice to be the reason for someone else's smile.

Showing that you value the people you care about is a good way to deepen your bonds. If you have friends you don't see often due to distance or busy schedules, giving them a reminder that you value them as a friend now and then is a good way to keep that friendship alive through absence of social interaction.

You want the people in your life to know that you appreciate them and that you care for them. Otherwise, it is easy for communication to cease and as life gets busier, your relationships drift apart. Part of having a high EQ is valuing others for their strengths and the impact they have on your life. So, show them that you do.

Make Respectful and Constructive Feedback

In previous sections, you were told that you should seek feedback from others. There is another side to that however, and that is providing feedback. This feedback might be something you give to a coworker, a friend, family member, or a significant other. However, just like when you get feedback, you want to give constructive and respectful feedback.

You want to express yourself clearly and directly but also with respect. This will help the other person understand where you are coming from and not feel attacked. You'll be using your self-awareness skills, self-management skills, and social awareness skills to determine what you want to give feedback on, how and why it impacts you, and the best way to give it without hurting the other person's feelings. You may need to write these things down in your emotional journal and adjust your methods and findings as necessary.

Feedback should be given face to face. This way you allow the other person to see your body language and your behavior as well as being able to see theirs clearly.

The best formula for constructive feedback is the XYZ formula. This is broken down to, "When you did X, I felt Y, and I would prefer if you did Z instead." This is a calm, non-accusatory way to phrase your feedback. You don't put the blame on a specific person and you offer a solution so it isn't just a complaint.

For example, you could say, "When you changed plans last minute to hang out with a friend instead of me, I felt angry and betrayed. I would have preferred if you had met with your friend at a different time."

There are situations where feedback is going to be uncomfortable, regardless of how respectful you are being. Not everyone likes to hear that they hurt someone else's feelings or that they angered them. It usually results in denial, defensiveness, and deflection.

Understanding that potential for backlash, you'll want to carefully consider the best way to approach these situations in a way to minimize that outcome but still get your point across.

Chapter 6:

Putting It Into Practice

Now that you know what you can to raise your EQ, it is time to make a plan for yourself so that you can use what you learned to begin benefitting yourself and achieving your goals. Please remember that change can be hard, especially when you are learning new skills and training your body and your mind to respond differently. A lot of it comes down to repetition, practicing the same skills over and over, improving your abilities every day. It is time to put into practice everything that you've learned and start seeing results!

It is commonly said that it takes 21 days to make a habit stick. With that in mind, each skill will take several weeks to ingrain in your mind and body, and that is only if you practice them every single day. Fortunately, you can work on several skills at a time. There will be plenty of opportunities every day that you can apply your new emotional intelligence tools to, and many of these opportunities allow you to practice more than one skill. Others are more situational and it could take even longer before you have the opportunity to really work on them. For example, practicing cultural social awareness is going to be based on how often you are exposed to other cultures.

If you are feeling overwhelmed or think that it is downright impossible, break it down into a step by step plan for yourself. Rather than focus on the overall goal and the big picture, try setting smaller goals for yourself. The best way to set a goal is to write down your overall goal, for example "increasing your chances of success". Then, you'll want to write down three steps to take in order to reach that goal, such as "improving EQ," "getting a better job," "establish a long-term romantic relationship." Once you have your three steps written out, break each of them into three smaller steps.

You'll have nine small steps to take that will then fulfill the three steps which will lead you to your overall goal. It might look like you have more to do, but if you focus on one or two of the smallest steps at a time, you'll be able to get through them much quicker. It takes less time, energy, and focus to achieve a small step than to fulfill a huge goal. So, break your goals down into easier steps, building a self-help plan that is designed around exactly what you want to accomplish.

A good place to start with setting small goals for yourself is to pick one of the components of emotional intelligence. These components are self-awareness, self-management, social awareness, and relationship management. If you don't know where to start, a good entry level point is with self-awareness since the other components and skills build off of your own self-awareness.

However, if you have already mastered self-awareness, or have already made strides in being aware of your thoughts, emotions, and reactions, you might want to start somewhere else. Wherever you start, keep in mind that the skills build off each other, and starting with relationship management before improving social awareness might not be as effective without the precursory knowledge. Unless you have already mastered self-awareness, self-management, and social awareness, it is not recommended that you begin working on relationship management until the other three aspects have been thoroughly improved.

Once you have your starting point, pick three of the skills and methods that are listed under that chapter topic to begin working on. Write down a plan for how to improve these skills as well as how you can incorporate them into your daily life. If they are based around events, come up with a list of events that are happening in the next three weeks, plan out how you can use your newly learned skills. When it comes down to it, these skills are like muscles. You have to keep exercising them so that they remain strong.

It is a good idea to select three skills that don't have a lot of crossovers and can't be used for the same situations. This way you can practice methods that will help you in many different areas. When you feel like you have a good handle on those three skills, if you think the emotional intelligence concept needs some more work, pick another three and begin working on them. You can choose to work on all the skills that are provided in each chapter section, or you can pick and choose the ones that are going to be most beneficial to you and your success.

After completing your first three, if you think you have a good handle on that particular concept, move onto the next one and pick three new skills to begin working on. Practice as many of the skills and methods as you need to feel comfortable in that area and then move onto the next one. Now, if you move on from one component, and then realize that you didn't get as far in it as you wanted, just go back and pick up another three topics from your previous concept of study. Don't view this as failure, because it isn't. Think of it as a pit stop. You've made a lot of progress, but you still need to refresh yourself now and then before you can keep moving forward.

Remember, your body and brain are literally being reprogrammed and rewired to react and behave differently. Every now and then, it might default to its previous programming. This is just a glitch in the system that can be worked through by refreshing yourself on the new programming. If you think that you already have a high self-awareness, and jump right into self-management, but then realize you don't have as much self-awareness as you originally thought, don't be discouraged. This whole process is a massive exercise in self-discovery and self-improvement. There is a lot you are going to learn about yourself, and isn't that the point? So, if you learn something you weren't expecting, make it work for you. Take it as a sign that your self-discovery is working!

Relationship management is worked on last because it is a culmination of all the skills and methods that you practice up until that point. It is a good ending point because it brings everything together and even has you expand on those techniques for more advanced uses. If relationship management is your only goal or the only area you need to improve on, you might still find it helpful to go through the list of skills and topics for self-awareness, self-management, and social awareness to see if there are any skills you need to brush up on before getting into relationship management.

During this time, it is a really good idea to take notes in your emotional journal. Keeping track of what works and what doesn't. This journal is going to be a major asset to you for self-reflection, reviewing your own progress and successes, and can become almost like your personal textbook or guide for gaining your own success. While you are working on improving your own EQ, don't be surprised if your overall goals, ambitions, or desires change with your personal growth. This happens a lot, because personal growth and change extend into all aspects of your life. Who you were when you started this journey wanted different things than the person you become by taking the journey. Make sure to update your goals and desires as you progress.

Your plan for raising your own EQ is going to be based a lot on your own lifestyle and what you are looking to gain from this process. Not everyone is going to have the same goals or the same areas to improve. That is why Chapters 4 and 5 offer so many different tools and skills to use. Tailor your plan around what you know you need to work on first. In the process, you might find other areas that could benefit from some improvement. On the flip side, you could discover that you are much better off in certain areas than you initially thought. Make sure to celebrate all your small victories and the milestones you reach. This will help keep you motivated to keep going.

The process of raising your EQ and changing the thought, behavior, and emotional patterns that you have been establishing for years, most of your life in fact, is going to take time and commitment. Don't expect to see progress immediately. Remember the skill of practicing delayed gratification? Making cognitive and behavioral changes are a great example of delayed gratification. That is going to apply to your progression through this self-help program. Results will happen, if you put the work, time, and effort in.

Hopefully, the desire to make yourself more successful, improving your relationships, and otherwise living the life you want to live are enough motivation for you to be excited and committed enough to stick with this course. If not, find something else that motivates you to succeed. To make this work, it has to be something you really want! Everyone has the ability to change their circumstances, they just need to want it.

Conclusion

Congratulations on completing your journey through *Emotional Intelligence: Build Strong Social Skills and Improve Your Relationships by Raising Your EQ With Proven Methods and Strategies.* By now, you should have all the knowledge and skills you need to begin practicing the proven methods that will increase your EQ. If you haven't already gotten yourself a notebook or journal, it is recommended that you get started with that and begin setting goals for yourself and applying what you've learned to your everyday life.

By improving your EQ, you have the chance to change your own circumstances. EQ is going to be the driving force that leads you to success. So, begin by defining success for yourself and then set some goals that you want to achieve that will make you successful. Take what you've learned about self-management, self-awareness, social awareness, and managing relationships and begin working towards your success.

Chapters 4 and 5 are going to be your core sources of information and knowledge to help you improve your EQ. They break down the concepts of self-awareness, self-management, social awareness, and relationship management into skills and tools that will help you improve in areas that are lacking. Use the information in these chapters to turn your weaknesses into strengths. Build your empathy and compassion so that your personal, professional, and familial relationships improve, growing stronger with a deeper emotional connection.

If you're in need of some good examples of why EQ is important and how it can impact your life, go back to Chapters 1, 2, and 3 to reread the anecdotes. Read them carefully and reflect on what about those stories you relate to and what doesn't seem to fit. Making this distinction will assist you in deciding what you need to work on most.

While the stories show extreme situations involving EQ and IQ, see how you can apply the same concepts that the stories present to your own life to get a better handle on where your EQ sits currently.

It is becoming generally accepted that IQ alone isn't enough to make someone successful. In order to achieve success and live the life you want, you'll need to stand out and make an impression. The kind of impression that you want to make is the kind that EQ helps with. Set yourself apart from your peers and show the world that you have something to offer. Research into the field of emotional intelligence is growing, and all the results support the notion that EQ is even more important to success than IQ. With that understanding, use the information in this book to change your life.

Raising your EQ is essentially like reprogramming your mind and body. It takes work, time, and effort. Being committed to this change is going to ensure progress and success. This kind of personal reprogramming isn't going to yield instant results. Stick with it, because when you do start seeing results, you are going to be blown away by the immense shifts in your life!

In the beginning of this book, you were promised that you would learn the skills and tools to raise your EQ and achieve your own success. Now, you have what you need to reach that goal. It is up to you to make a plan for yourself and get the ball rolling. This process is meant to empower you, which means that it relies on your personal power, choices, and effort to happen.

You might even find it helpful to find a free EQ test online, there are several available on different websites. The tests don't boast perfect accuracy, but it can help you understand what you need to work on most. Once you know the area or areas that require the most attention, you'll be able to develop a personal plan that helps you build the skills you need to improve that area. If the test results seem confusing, maybe try a different test. Or, look at the documentation provided by the test host to see what tips they offer for understanding your test results. Global Leadership Foundation has a fairly quick EQ test with plenty of additional information to help you interpret what your scores are.

The greatest take away for you to remember after you put this book down is that your emotions are not good or bad. Your emotions are necessary to survival and to success. It is within your power to manage your emotions and use them as assets in your life. After learning about self-awareness, self-management, social awareness, and relationship management, it all comes back to your own emotions and how you manage them.

Everything that you learned from reading this book is interconnected with how you can increase your EQ and your success. It is your choice what you take away from the book and how you intend to use this knowledge. Self-help is all about guiding you to your own potential. That is exactly what you have been offered, a chance to reach your potential and benefit from it.

So, don't forget that by increasing your EQ, you change your thought patterns, behavioral patterns, and emotional responses. These three chemical, physiological, and biological impulses are automatic responses to particular stimuli. Even though they are automatic, you can still train your body and mind to alter what reactions it defaults to when exposed to stimuli. There are plenty of reasons to choose to improve your EQ, and only a few reasons not to. Has there ever been a better time to make all your goals happen?

Thank you for your support in reading *Emotional Intelligence*. Your contribution is greatly appreciated. If you enjoyed this book and learned some great new tools to use, please leave a positive review so that this book can continue to spread and help others the same way it helped you. In all honesty, there is plenty more for you to learn and a lot more information that can be used to help you gain the most from your experience with practicing the methods provided in this book. Good luck on your personal growth journey!

References

About emotional intelligence. (2019). *About emotional intelligence.* TalentSmart. https://www.talentsmart.com/about/emotional-intelligence.php

Bariso, Justin. (2020). *13 signs of high emotional intelligence.* Inc. https://www.inc.com/justin-bariso/13-things-emotionally-intelligent-people-do.html

Cherry, Kendra. (Jan 2020). *The 6 types of basic emotions and their effect on human behavior.* Verywellmind. https://www.verywellmind.com/an-overview-of-the-types-of-emotions-4163976

Cherry Kendra. (May 2020). *The purpose of our emotions.* Verywellmind. https://www.verywellmind.com/the-purpose-of-emotions-2795181

Emotional intelligence. (n.d.). *Emotional intelligence.* Global leadership foundation. https://globalleadershipfoundation.com/deepening-understanding/emotional-intelligence/

EQ Vs. IQ. (2020). *EQ Vs. IQ.* Diffen. https://www.diffen.com/difference/EQ_vs_IQ

How to improve emotional intelligence: 10 tips for increasing self-awareness. (n.d.). *How to improve emotional intelligence: 10 tips for increasing self-awareness.* sixseconds. https://www.6seconds.org/2018/02/27/emotional-intelligence-tips-awareness

Improving emotional intelligence (EQ). (1999-2020). *Improving emotional intelligence (EQ).* HelpGuide.

https://www.helpguide.org/articles/mental-health/emotional-intelligence-eq.htm

Keyser, John. (June 2013). *Emotional intelligence is key to our success.* ADT. https://www.td.org/insights/emotional-intelligence-is-key-to-our-success

McCarney, RW Schulz, J & Grey, AR. (2012). *Effectiveness of mindfulness-based therapies in reducing symptoms of depression: a meta-analysis.* Taylor and Francis online. https://www.tandfonline.com/doi/abs/10.1080/13642537.2012.713186

Merriam-Webster. (n.d.). Emotion. In *Merriam-Webster.com dictionary.* https://www.merriam-webster.com/dictionary/emotion

Nelis, Delphine Quoidbach, Jordi Mikolajczak, Moira Hansenne, & Michel, (July 2009). *Increasing emotional intelligence: (how) is it possible?* ScienceDirect. https://www.sciencedirect.com/science/article/abs/pii/S0191886909000567

The global EI test results. (n.d.). *The global EI test results.* Global leadership foundation. https://globalleadershipfoundation.com/cgi-bin/eiscore.pl

What is emotional intelligence? (2020). *What is emotional intelligence?* Institute for health and human potential. https://www.ihhp.com/meaning-of-emotional-intelligence/

Printed in Great Britain
by Amazon